TEMPLE BAR — DUBLIN

AN ILLUSTRATED HISTORY

BY

PAT LIDDY

ACKNOWLEDGEMENTS

There are many people who should be thanked most sincerely for helping me over countless hurdles in putting this volume together. It would be impossible to name everyone and in any case, even if I attempted to, I fear I would have omitted unintentionally some names. I will mention a representative panel and ask all others to believe that I am indebted to them.

I must first thank the people of Temple Bar Properties who actively supported and encouraged this book from the start and in particular I want to single out Belinda Buckley and Lisa Tinley.

To the many people who gave me cuttings, manuscripts, maps, records and any other item of interest which were woven into the tapestry, my gratitude. Again I will mention but a few; Pat Wallace, Director of the National Museum, Prof. Howard Clarke of UCD, Colm Lennon of Maynooth College and Douglas Hyde of Dublin County Council.

I would like to thank the staff of the following institutions: Dr. Pat Donlon, Director of the National Library and Elizabeth Kirwan and Phil McCann of the National Library; Adrian le Harivel, the National Gallery; Tom O'Connor and Philip of the Civic Museum; Mary Clark of Dublin Corporation Archives and Pat Russell of Dublin Corporation Development Department; David Griffin of the Irish Architectural Archive; and Maire Kennedy of the Gilbert Library who suggested the use of The Freeman's Journal extracts.

Without the help and patience of all the owners and staff of the many businesses in Temple Bar whom I approached, this book would have been a non-starter.

My thanks to two authorities on Dublin's history; Eamonn MacThomais and long-time resident of Temple Bar Pat Casey, who brought me around the streets broad and narrow.

Not forgetting Rory and Donal McNeela of Oisin Arts who helped at the layout stages, the staff of Cahill Printers including Linda Alvarez, John Mullally and Matt Kilburn. Brian McManus of Summit Graphics, Barry O'Brien of Irish Platemaking Services and Louise Briscoe who went on several errands for me to the Temple Bar area.

Thanks to Bernard Loughlin and all at the Tyrone Gutherie Centre at Annamakerrig for peace and quiet during a few weeks work there.

Finally, everlasting thanks to my wife Josephine — if I said she typed my manuscript it would be a gross understatement — and to my patient children Anne Marie, Brendan and Padraig who saw their Dad in body only while his spirit was elsewhere for several weeks.

TEMPLE BAR — DUBLIN

DEDICATION

To everyone with a vision for Dublin.

First Published in Ireland in 1992 by
Temple Bar Properties Ltd.
14/19 Crow Street
Dublin 2.

Text © Pat Liddy and Temple Bar Properties Ltd.

Illustrations and Photographs © Pat Liddy (except as ascribed)

Cover design © Pat Liddy

Colour Transparencies: Summit Graphics Ltd., Dublin.

Colour Plates: Irish Platemaking Services Ltd., Dublin.

Index compiled by Helen Litton.

Typeset and Printed by Cahill Printers Ltd., Dublin.

Hardbound ISBN 1 874202 04 4

Paperbound ISBN 1 874202 03 6

FOREWORD

The current restoration and refurbishment of the Temple Bar area and its development as Dublin's Cultural Quarter is giving a new dimension to the streets, buildings and very fabric of the area. This renewal process has inspired an examination of the fascinating history of the area. It has also prompted a realisation of the importance of recording for future generations the history of what was once, and is set to become again, a truly significant cultural and architectural resource, and a vibrant, colourful and living part of our city.

This book, *Temple Bar — Dublin, An Illustrated History by Pat Liddy,* is the first comprehensive history of the area ever to be published. The history of the area puts the Temple Bar development firmly into context, both in terms of its past and its future. It is important that the people who live in, work in and visit Temple Bar have a sense and an appreciation of that history.

This is a wonderfully illustrated, interesting and enlightening journey through time which provides us with a true sense of what life was like in this special Quarter of Dublin since pre-Viking times. All credit must go to Pat Liddy for his tireless research and dedication to the preservation of our past.

Albert Reynolds, T.D.
An Taoiseach

TEMPLE BAR PROPERTIES LIMITED

Temple Bar Properties is the government-established company set up in 1991 to oversee the development of the Temple Bar area and the creation of Dublin's Cultural Quarter. This is a unique urban renewal project which will build on what has already taken place spontaneously in the area resulting in a bustling cultural, residential and small business precinct of charm and distinction to be enjoyed by Irish people and visitors alike. The project is scheduled for completion in 1996.

We recognise the importance, at this early stage of the project, of compiling and documenting a comprehensive record of the history of this very special area which dates back to pre-Viking days and we are delighted to be the publishers of this important work. We would like to pay a warm tribute to Pat Liddy who took this task on board with such enthusiasm and care resulting in this fascinating publication.

We hope you, the reader, will capture in the following pages, the rich history that surrounds us in this unique part of old Dublin.

Laura Magahy
Managing Director,
Temple Bar Properties Ltd.

TEMPLE BAR PROPERTIES

CONTENTS

		Page
Introduction … … … … … … … … … … … … …		9
Chapter One The Earliest Days … … … … … … … … … … …		11
Chapter Two The New Order … … … … … … … … … … …		19
Chapter Three Breaking Free … … … … … … … … … … …		27
Chapter Four Obedientia Civium Urbis Felicitas … … … … … … … …		41
Chapter Five Streets Broad and Narrow … … … … … … … … …		73
Bibliography … … … … … … … … … … … …		147
Index… … … … … … … … … … … … …		148

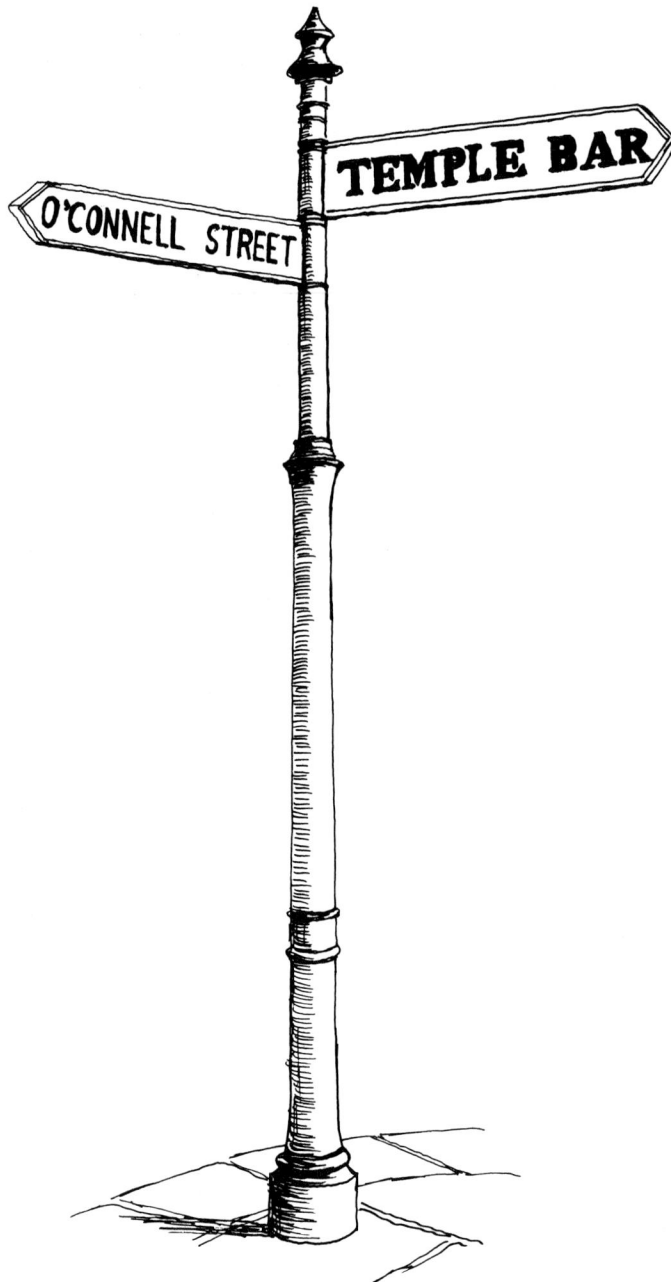

INTRODUCTION

Sir William Temple (1555-1627) had come to Ireland in 1599 as secretary to Robert Devereux, the Earl of Essex. He was elected Provost of Trinity College in 1609.

His grandson was also called Sir William Temple (1628-1699). He was elected Member of Parliament for Carlow in 1662 and held the position of Master of the Rolls. Their descendants included First Lords of the Treasury, Secretaries of State, Keepers of the Privy Seal, First Lords of the Admiralty and a Prime Minister.

Where and what is Temple Bar and why is it so called? Strictly speaking Temple Bar is a short, modest city-centre street near the south banks of the river Liffey. In itself the street has no great significance or historical connections but in the last few years the Temple Bar area has taken on a national prominence and has become a byword for urban regeneration, restoration and cultural development.

Temple Bar was ostensibly named after Sir William Temple whose residence and gardens previously stood on the site in the early 17th century. However, as there was already a Temple Bar leading onto Fleet Street in London, it might be correctly supposed that these names were imported both as a memory of England's Capital (the native city of many of Dublin's administrators and developers) and at the same time to co-incidentally honour the well-regarded Temple family. The earliest record of Temple Bar on a map of Dublin is 1673.

A "bar," originally barr, is an estuary sandbank or, as in the case of the London version, a barrier or gate blocking the entrance to the city.

Today Temple Bar is taken to mean the area bordered by Fishamble, Dame and Westmoreland Streets and Wellington Quay. It has been given a special status for building and residential renewal and development as a Cultural Quarter by legislation and tax incentives.

From the 1950's this whole area began to decline as businesses and shoppers moved elsewhere. From 1981, C.I.E. (the state transport company) started to buy up property to build a transportation centre. However, the plan ran into difficulties and while awaiting a resolution C.I.E. leased out premises at low rents which attracted creative and fringe activities. These, in turn, breathed new life into the area.

The upsurge in a whole range of activities brought a fresh focus to the charming characteristics of Temple Bar and after intensive lobbying by various groups including the Temple Bar Development Council and the preparation of an Action Plan by Dublin Corporation, the government took decisive action by introducing the Temple Bar Area Renewal and Development Act.

Opportunities now exist for Temple Bar to relate to the essence of each stage of its colourful past, a past that was inextricably bound up with the genesis and development of Dublin.

The rest will be history.

Pat Liddy
November 1992.

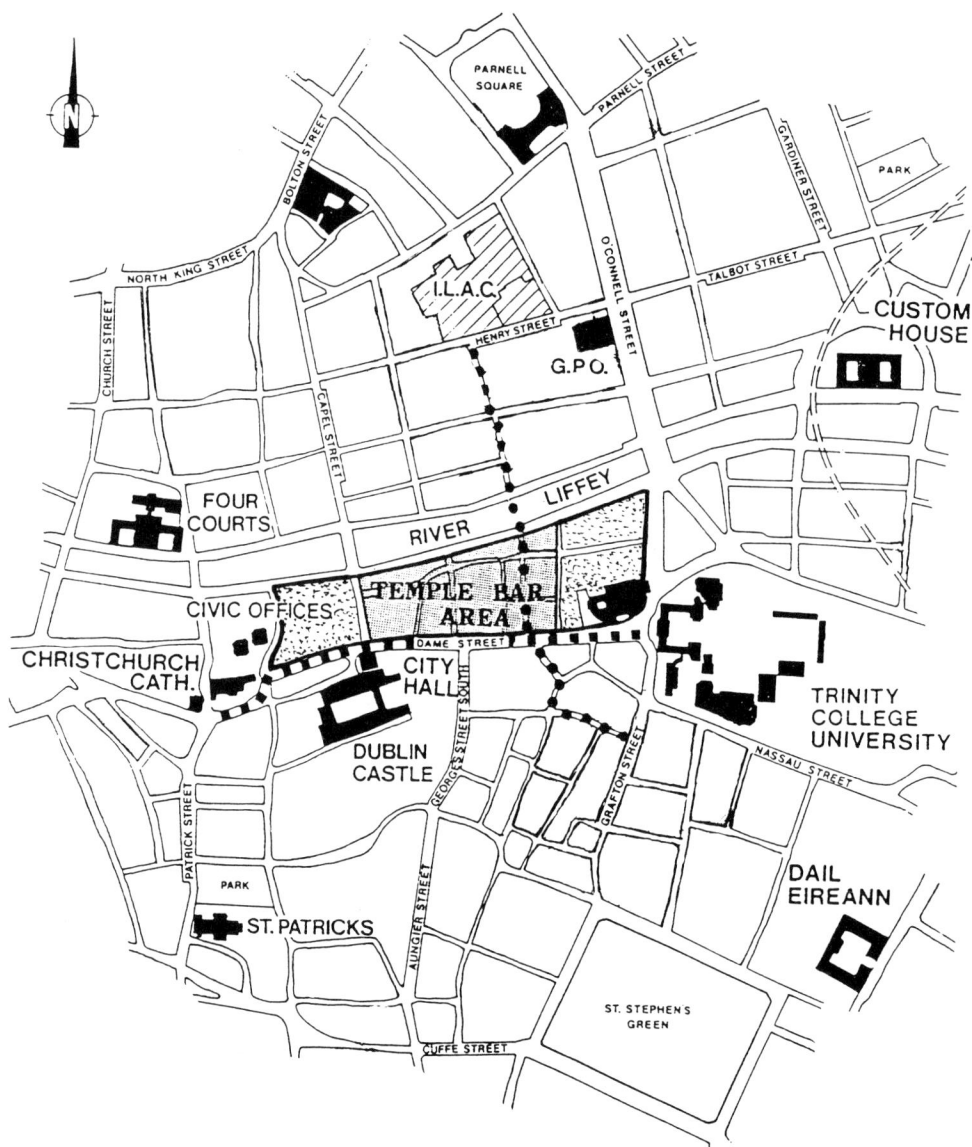

Chapter 1

THE EARLIEST DAYS

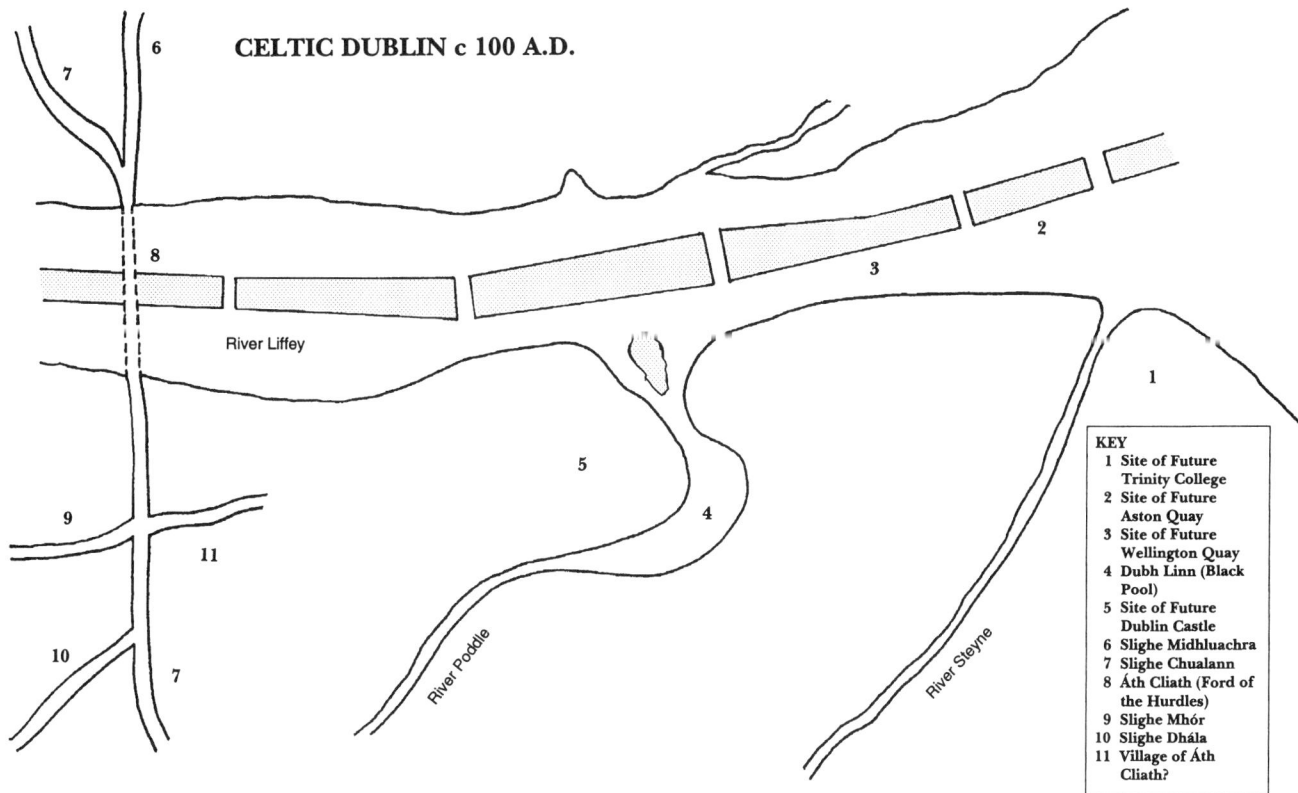

CELTIC DUBLIN c 100 A.D.

KEY
1 Site of Future Trinity College
2 Site of Future Aston Quay
3 Site of Future Wellington Quay
4 Dubh Linn (Black Pool)
5 Site of Future Dublin Castle
6 Slighe Midhluachra
7 Slighe Chualann
8 Áth Cliath (Ford of the Hurdles)
9 Slighe Mhór
10 Slighe Dhála
11 Village of Áth Cliath?

River Liffey

River Poddle

River Steyne

Notice how wide the Liffey is at this time but on the other hand it is quite a shallow river especially at low tide and it was easily crossed by men and animals at the Ford of the Hurdles (Áth Cliath).

We know that mesolithic man probed and hunted around the Dublin region perhaps as far back as 6,000 B.C. Fishermen of 7,000 years ago have left us remains of their cooking on Dalkey Island.

Technological progress in the shape of tools and farming practices marked the arrival of the neolithic people 1,000 years later and within the next millennium tiny settlements grew up along the Liffey Valley. About 3,000 years ago the Bronze Age dawned in Dublin and sites from this period abound including those at Parliament Street and at Suffolk Street near College Green.

While these ancient and sophisticated civilisations waxed and waned and left little evidence of why they ultimately vanished, the arrival of the Celts around 300 B.C. heralded a new and more important era for Dublin. Within the space of three more centuries Dublin had assumed a strategic importance as the crossroads of the country's main Celtic highways. These four routes converged on Dublin with the two northern roads crossing the Liffey at the Ford of the Hurdles or Áth Cliath, the name the city was to adopt as the official Irish language version. The ford was located just beyond Merchants' Quay.

A community of sorts must have formed around Áth Cliath, at least to provide hospitality and supplies to weary travellers. As yet no remains of a village have been found at the site but it could be said that the story of Temple Bar and, of course, of Dublin really begins at this time.

The Four Ancient Highways were:

Slighe Mhór;	Ran from present High Street to Galway along a natural causeway called the Esker Riada.
Slighe Dála;	Started from the Coombe to end in Limerick.
Slighe Chualann;	Connected Tara to Wicklow.
Slighe Midhluachra;	The second northern road linked Derry with Waterford.

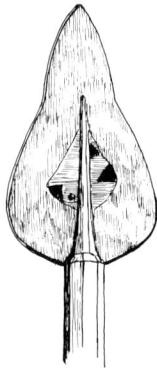

Bronze Spearhead
Iron Age
National Museum

Bronze Shield
700 B.C.
National Museum

Beaded Bronze Collar
Late First Century A.D.
National Museum

Bronze Scabbard Mount
First Century A.D.
National Museum

(Note: The following series of maps will focus solely on the topography of the area of Dublin now known as Temple Bar and will be referred to as such even though, as a geographical definition, it is of recent origin).

CHRISTIAN DUBLIN c 800 A.D.

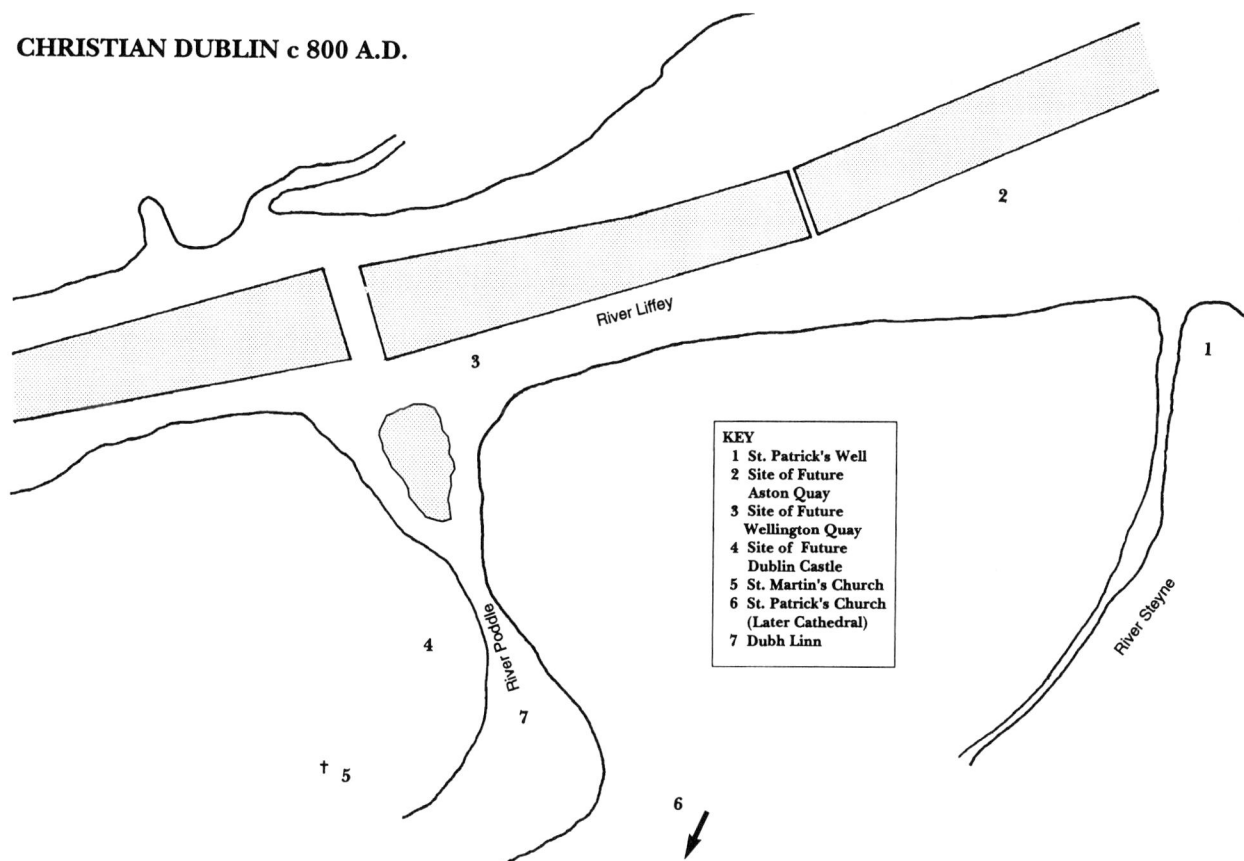

River Liffey

River Poddle

River Steyne

KEY
1 St. Patrick's Well
2 Site of Future
  Aston Quay
3 Site of Future
  Wellington Quay
4 Site of Future
  Dublin Castle
5 St. Martin's Church
6 St. Patrick's Church
  (Later Cathedral)
7 Dubh Linn

Undoubtedly, a scattering of people must have lived here — a few farmers or fishermen, perhaps — but virtually nothing remains of any historical or architectural interest. A well (one of several in Dublin) named after Saint Patrick was sited near the present-day Trinity College. The pool "Dubh Linn" (Black Pool) where the river Poddle just meets the Liffey gave us the name Dublin.

The Celts were warlike (when not farming) but mainly on a factional basis. Legend records that raiding parties of one sort or another passed through or bivouaced in the general Dublin area but there are no tales of campaigns or attempts to control the Ford of the Hurdles until 770.

Christianity came into this relatively peaceful place about 450 when St. Patrick reputedly baptised a local chieftain and his people at a well now marked by a table in the park beside St. Patrick's Cathedral. The saint's mission was obviously successful for a number of important monasteries were founded in the vicinity, especially at Glasnevin and Tallaght.

By 800 A.D. a number of small celtic churches had been built around the perimeter of Temple Bar. They included Cill Céle Crist (later Christ Church Cathedral), St. Colum Cille (later St.

Audeon's), St. Doulagh's (later St. Olaf's), St. Martin's (beside Dublin Castle) and St. Mac Tail's (just south of the castle).

These churches, along with some others and the adjacent monasteries must suggest that there was a reasonable population in the region even if it was spread out thinly. The creation of a diocese was justified by 660 when Dublin's first bishop, St. Wiro, was consecrated. Others would hear of the relative stability, wealth and strategic advantage of the bay area and would arrive to change the balance of power not only in Dublin but widely throughout the country. The Age of the Vikings was dawning.

St. Doulagh's, Malahide Road.
The original church stood at the bottom of Fishamble Street before moving out to the suburbs c 1160.

VIKING MAP c 1000

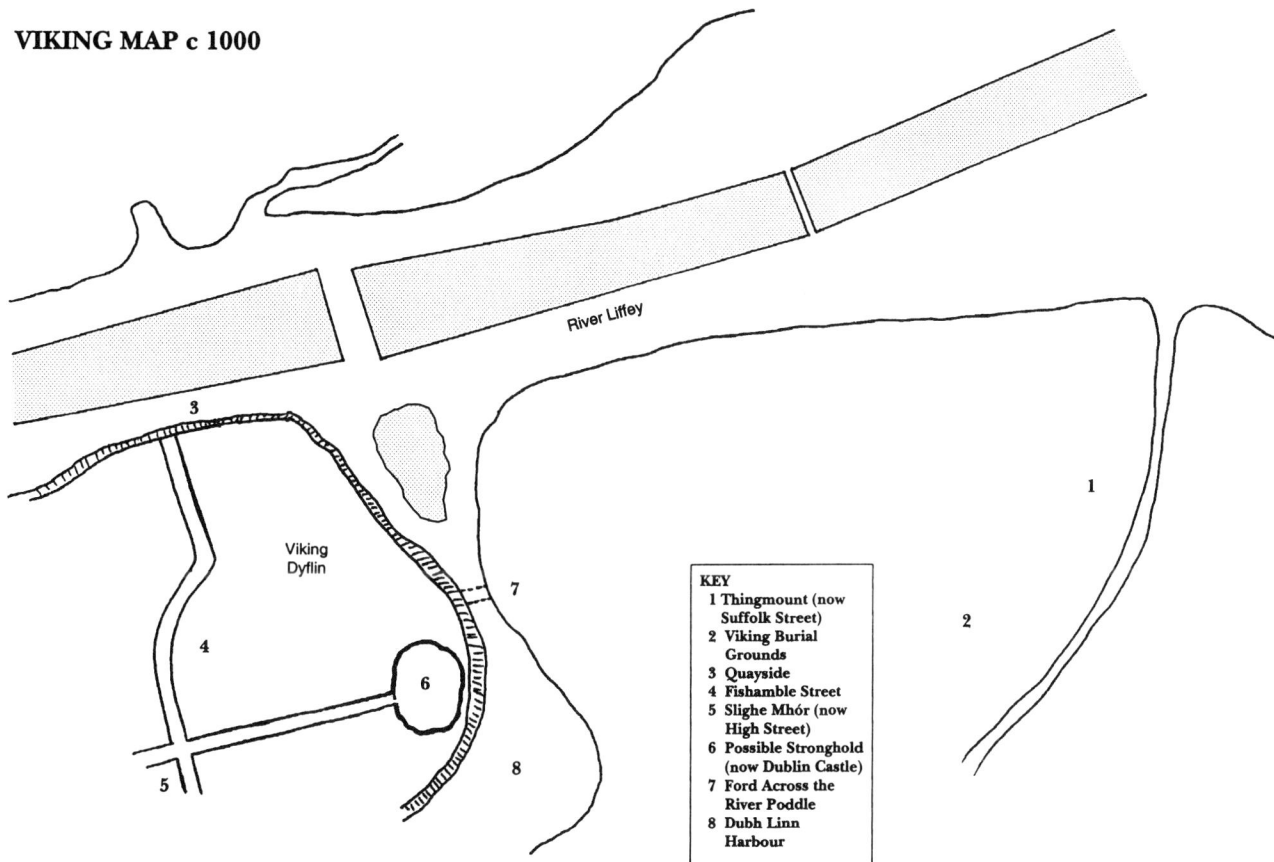

Viking
Dyflin

River Liffey

3

7

4

6

5

8

1

2

KEY
1 Thingmount (now
   Suffolk Street)
2 Viking Burial
   Grounds
3 Quayside
4 Fishamble Street
5 Slighe Mhór (now
   High Street)
6 Possible Stronghold
   (now Dublin Castle)
7 Ford Across the
   River Poddle
8 Dubh Linn
   Harbour

The Fair Headed Foreigners

The first encounter native Dubliners had with the Fionn Gaill (the fair-headed foreigners — giving us the name of Fingal for North County Dublin) was brutal and short. Commando-style, efficient longboats beached on Lambay Island and disgorged their Viking occupants who quickly sacked the monastery and carried off their booty. That was in the year 795.

For the next four decades, no settlement or monastic community was safe from surprise attack from marauding Norsemen. Not that the monasteries were the exclusive prey of the Ostmen (men from the east), Irish war lords ravaged these seats of learning and prayer with as much ferocity and frequency as their new rivals from overseas.

Requiring a more settled base for their expeditions and expanding commercial activities, a decision was made around the council fires in far-off Norway to invade and occupy a suitable anchorage in Ireland. In 837 an impressive fleet of sixty-five Viking ships capable of carrying up to 3,000 warriors, craftsmen and family members sailed up the river Liffey. They erected a long stone, a symbol of their intention to stay, on the shore near where Pearse and D'Olier Streets meet today. A tentative settlement was made further upriver but the Vikings deferred a permanent landing for the moment.

In 841 they established a fortified harbour or longphort, and erected a stockade. For the next sixty years onslaughts from the Irish and rivalries within the Viking nation would make their hold on their modest territorial gains more tenuous. By 902 they were driven from the shores but within fifteen years King Sitric II reoccupied Dublin, this time at the site of the Dubh Linn. The Vikings were now here to stay but not without frequent challenges and some defeats at the hands of the native Irish.

It is from the period of Sitric II's reign that large scale earthen ramparts were thrown up around the small Norse community and an urban lifestyle developed. The events and struggles among the Irish kings in their quest for regional or national supremacy was to embroil the Vikings over the next three centuries and would eventually lead to their defeat and banishment across the river by the Normans.

Viking Finds

One of Europe's largest urban excavations started in High Street in 1962 and continued into Christchurch Place, Winetavern Street and Fishamble Street before concluding in 1981. It yielded a greater and more important find of Viking artefacts than any other site including those of York, London, Hamburg and Bergin.

The drawing includes a small iron saw, shaped to resemble a Viking Longboat. It was used to cut bone and antler, as in the examples shown of an 11th-century comb and its carrying case. The Norsemen are credited with introducing the composite comb into Ireland. The comb consists of two side plates between which are gripped a number of individual tooth plates. Antler pegs, iron or copper rivets hold the whole assembly together.

Imported from abroad, the iron sword is 12th-century. The polished bone pins, most likely used to tie up hair or fasten garments, have finely decorated heads which represent real or mythological animals. Also unearthed were hundreds of lead weights, all conforming to units based on the Carolingian ounce. Both folding and rigid scales were used to weigh precious metals. The example here features a 12th-century beam and 13th-century pans. An iron slave collar shows another side of Viking commerce — the export of Irish labour.

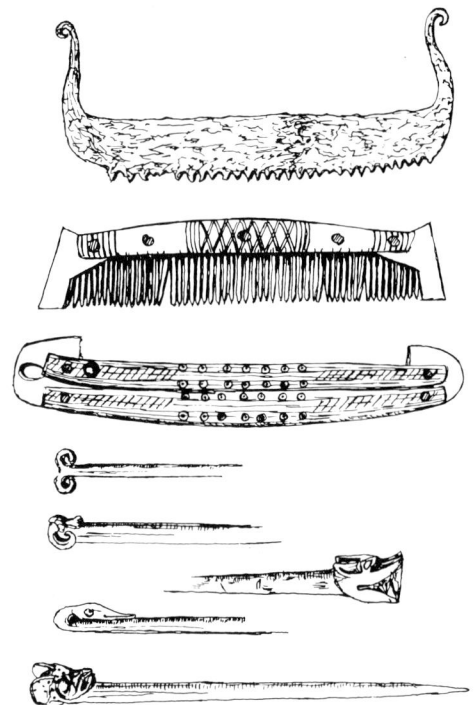

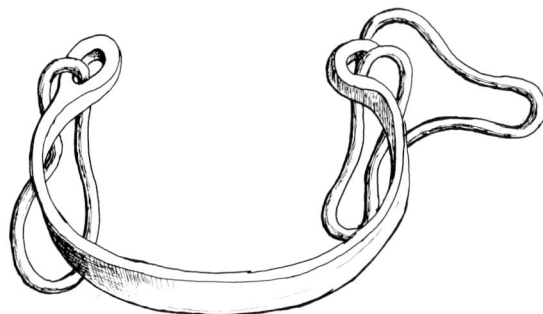

16

Viking Longship

In 1988 a full size replica of a Viking Longship, the "Dyflin", (built by the East Wall Watersports Group) was launched in the old Liffey Dockyard. Never intended as a museum piece, the boat is used as a local community training vessel and can often be seen on the River Liffey, even upriver as far as the Halfpenny Bridge.

Standing on board the surprisingly large deck, it becomes easy to reflect on the awesome skills and capabilities of the Vikings. Copied exactly from the burial mound ship discovered at Gokstad in Norway, the Dublin vessel is 76 feet (23 metres) long, has a 42 feet (12.8 metres) high mast and is equipped with 32 oars (plus 8 spares for safety). Taking a draught of only three feet (1 metre), the ship slices through the water at six knots per hour when powered by oars and at double this speed under sail.

The Longship, with its shallow draught, allowed the easy passage up the shallow Liffey. Then, by its seaworthiness and reliability, it extended the range and influence of the Vikings from Greenland to Russia and from Norway to Africa making Dublin a relatively important and wealthy hub of an enormous empire.

Inside Viking Dyflin

After the extensive excavations in the Fishamble Street and Wood Quay areas between 1974 and 1981, archaeologists are now able to reconstruct fairly accurately what Viking Dyflin must have looked like and what kind of lives the inhabitants led.

The tenth century town was approximately 16 acres (6.5 hectares) in size and was surrounded by a high ditch surmounted by a post-and-wattle palisade. By the twelfth century a stone wall protected the town. Streets, topped by gravel, logs or woven wattle mats, led to the waterfront gates. Minor laneways served the streets. Fish was landed at the Fyssche Slyppe (a later medieval term) at the bottom of Fishamble Street. Merchants, jewellers and wood carvers also peopled this street.

While the king may have resided in a large defended thatched house, likely to have been located on the site of later Dublin Castle, the ordinary townsfolk lived more humbly. The house form seems to have been adapted from the existing Irish styles and methods. Generally, they were rectangular in shape and the thatched roof was supported by posts driven into the ground. The walls were post and wattle and may sometimes have been daubed with dung and other substances to keep out draughts.

Inside, a fire was lit in the centre aisle with the smoke evacuating through a hole in the roof. The side aisles were raised up for use as beds, seats and understorage. Doors were planked or made of wattle.

Many craftsmen such as combmakers, wood carvers, brooch-makers, leather-workers, weavers etc. worked from home while their wives prepared meals of thin bread and boiled meat and fish with nuts and fruit for dessert.

Life was difficult and dirty to say the least. Fleas, lice, smoke, cold and dampness added to the misery of crude hygiene and uncontrolled disease. Life expectancy was no more than the forties. It is a constant wonder that not only did this town survive — it appears to have thrived.

Chapter 2

THE NEW ORDER

ANGLO NORMAN DUBLIN c 1200

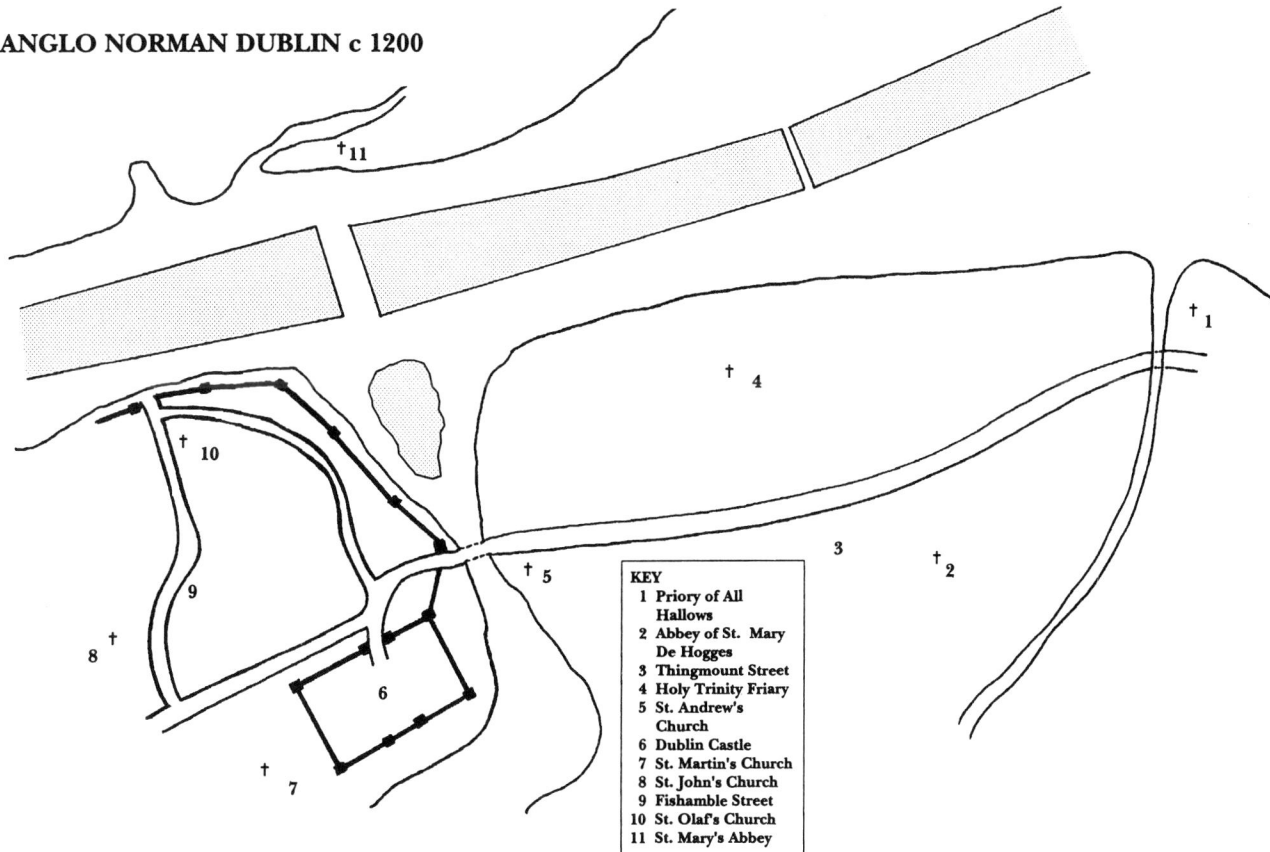

KEY
1. Priory of All Hallows
2. Abbey of St. Mary De Hogges
3. Thingmount Street
4. Holy Trinity Friary
5. St. Andrew's Church
6. Dublin Castle
7. St. Martin's Church
8. St. John's Church
9. Fishamble Street
10. St. Olaf's Church
11. St. Mary's Abbey

As has already been alluded to, it was the result of a bitter feud between the Irish themselves that introduced a new lordship over Dublin.

Dermot MacMurrough had lost the throne of Leinster and so he connived with Henry II of England to win it back. In return for military help MacMurrough promised the allegiance of Leinster to Henry and his daughter's hand to Richard FitzGilbert de Clare (Strongbow), the leader of the Norman invaders.

In 1170 a small but well equipped Norman army reached the gates of Dublin after a successful overland expedition. Norse King Hasculf tried to parley but while negotiations were underway some Normans gained entry to the town and their superior arms easily put down any resistance. Dublin was theirs and the majority of the Norse inhabitants fled the town and settled on the opposite side of the river Liffey.

The Normans began to consolidate their grip on the town and soon rebuilt and strengthened the defences. Lest they got too independently powerful, King Henry II arrived in Dublin in 1172 to assert his authority and by Royal Charter gave the city as a gift to the men of Bristol.

Dublin now began to take on its early medieval shape. New christian foundations appeared both inside and outside the walls. The population grew apace but for security reasons most people remained within the walls. Languages spoken in Dublin included English, French and Irish with some Welsh, Norse and the tongues of visiting merchants thrown in for good measure.

A proper municipal organisation, based on Royal Charters and the administration codes of the Anglo-Normans, was put into place. In 1192 Dublin Corporation was founded by a Charter of Prince John which allowed the citizens "to have all their reasonable guilds".

The City Walls

When the Normans invaded Dublin in 1170 the town was already walled. Over the next four centuries stronger walls, gates and towers were built and various extensions were made especially on the river front where a process of land reclamation from the Liffey, started by the Vikings, was continued. Two lines of walls faced the river which clearly demonstrates the amount of land won back from the water.

From time to time the walls fell into disrepair but news of some impending threat usually led to an urgent rebuilding programme. By the end of the sixteenth century the walls finally fell into disuse.

7. St. Audeon's Arch, Cook Street.
The city's last remaining gate.

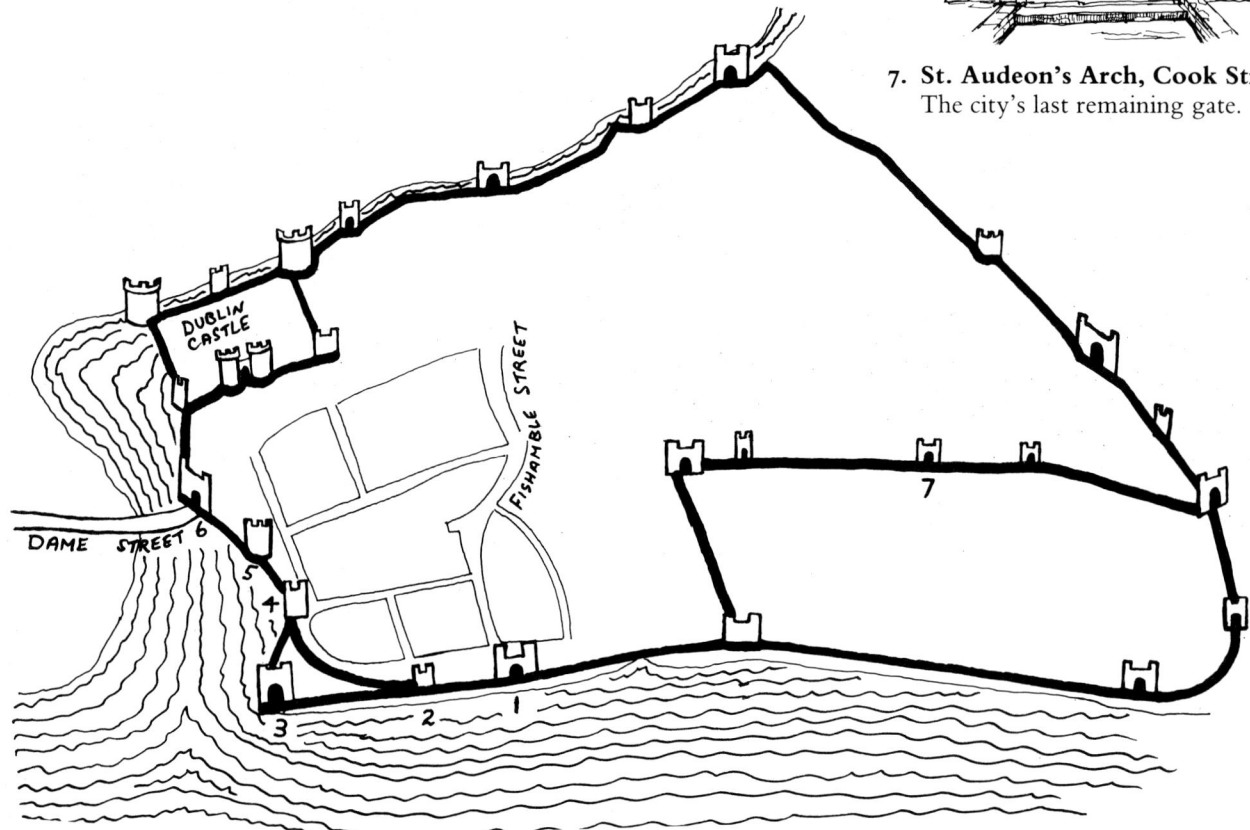

The towers and gates in the Temple Bar area.

1. Fyan's or Proudfoot's Castle.	3. Isolde's Tower.	5. Bise's Tower.
2. Case's Tower.	4. Buttevant's Tower.	6. Dame's Gate.

THE MIDDLE AGES (1300 – 1599)

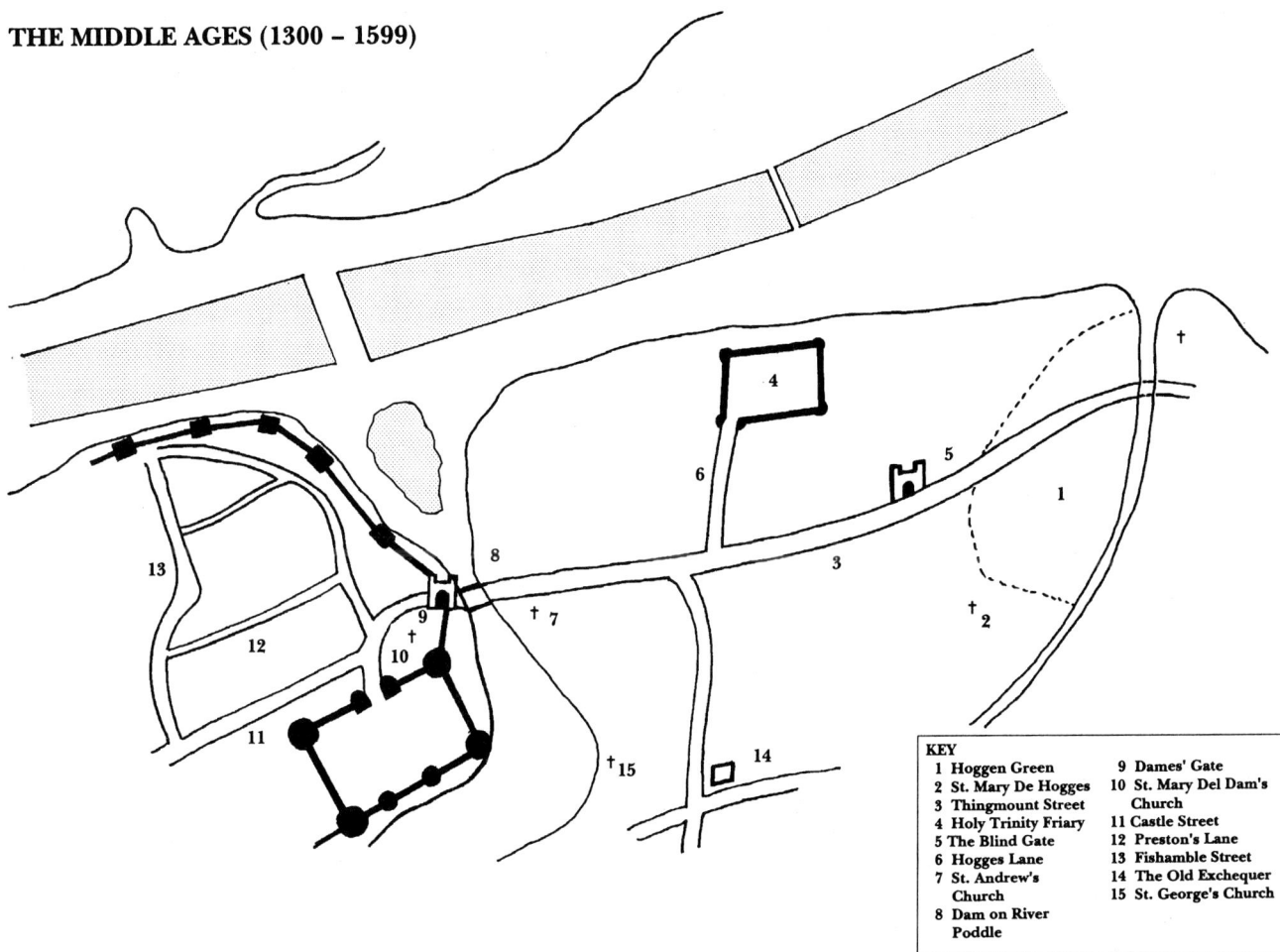

KEY
1 Hoggen Green
2 St. Mary De Hogges
3 Thingmount Street
4 Holy Trinity Friary
5 The Blind Gate
6 Hogges Lane
7 St. Andrew's Church
8 Dam on River Poddle
9 Dames' Gate
10 St. Mary Del Dam's Church
11 Castle Street
12 Preston's Lane
13 Fishamble Street
14 The Old Exchequer
15 St. George's Church

The start of the fourteenth century was not particularly auspicious for Dublin or its harassed citizens. Resentment of the Anglo-Normans grew among the native population and several clans in the nearby mountains carried out aggressive forays on the unprotected southern suburbs.

A more menacing threat loomed in 1317 when Edward Bruce attempted to take Dublin with an army of 20,000 men. Urgent defensive measures applied by the inhabitants successfully warded off the danger and Bruce retreated. However, over the next two centuries there were more assaults on the city but each time the aggressors were repulsed.

Devastation of the population came more from natural disasters than from wars. The population was decimated several times by plagues, diseases and famines, most notably by the Black Death in 1347 when over a third of the population of 12,000 was wiped out. To help ameliorate the lot of the unfortunate population (except the native Irish who were considered second class citizens), the town's water supply was greatly modernised, street paving was laid down, buildings were improved and the truculent mountain families were forcibly tamed.

Commerce increased and new dockside facilities, complete with a city crane, were built at Merchants' Quay. The second half of the sixteenth century was very busy for dockers. Trade in commodities such as wine prospered and traffic markedly increased between Dublin and the ports of Chester, Liverpool and Bristol.

Whenever possible, entertainment of one sort or another was encouraged to divert people away from their daily grind. Plays, pageants, jousting and archery contests took place in Hoggen (College) Green, a common grazing area just west of the walls and in front of All Hallows Priory (later Trinity College). Citizens relished getting away from the unhealthy confines of the enclosed city but a weather-eye always had to be kept out for personal safety when away from the comparative security of the fortifications.

In an era where people were accustomed to death an event occurred in 1596 which stunned the city and caused the first major shift eastwards into Temple Bar proper. A major revolt was sweeping through Ulster and shipments of arms and explosives were arriving into Dublin for the English troops. While barrels of gunpowder were being offloaded, a spark ignited a barrel causing

a massive explosion and fireball which consumed and flattened scores of buildings from Winetavern Street to Fishamble Street and killed one hundred and twenty men, women and children. The heart went out of the old town which never fully recovered and developers looked towards the possibilities now opening up outside the walls especially since the foundation of Trinity College in 1592.

The wattle, wicker and thatched houses of early medieval Dublin quickly gave way to more substantive timber framed houses in the 16th century. The residents of Fishamble Street were able to see the city's first public clocks erected in 1560 on the towers of the Tholsel, and Dublin Castle. However, living conditions were still not much better. The closely packed houses were easily consumed by fire. Hygiene at home and in public places was primitive to say the least. Space was so limited for building that houses were constructed right up to church and city walls. No respite from these circumstances could be found until the next century when expansion beyond the walls into districts like Temple Bar was achieved.

View of an Old House in Castle Street corner of Werburgh Street, taken down in April 1812.

Cage-work house, Castle Street.
The last timber framed "cage-work" house left standing in Dublin. It stood in Castle Street and was demolished in 1812.

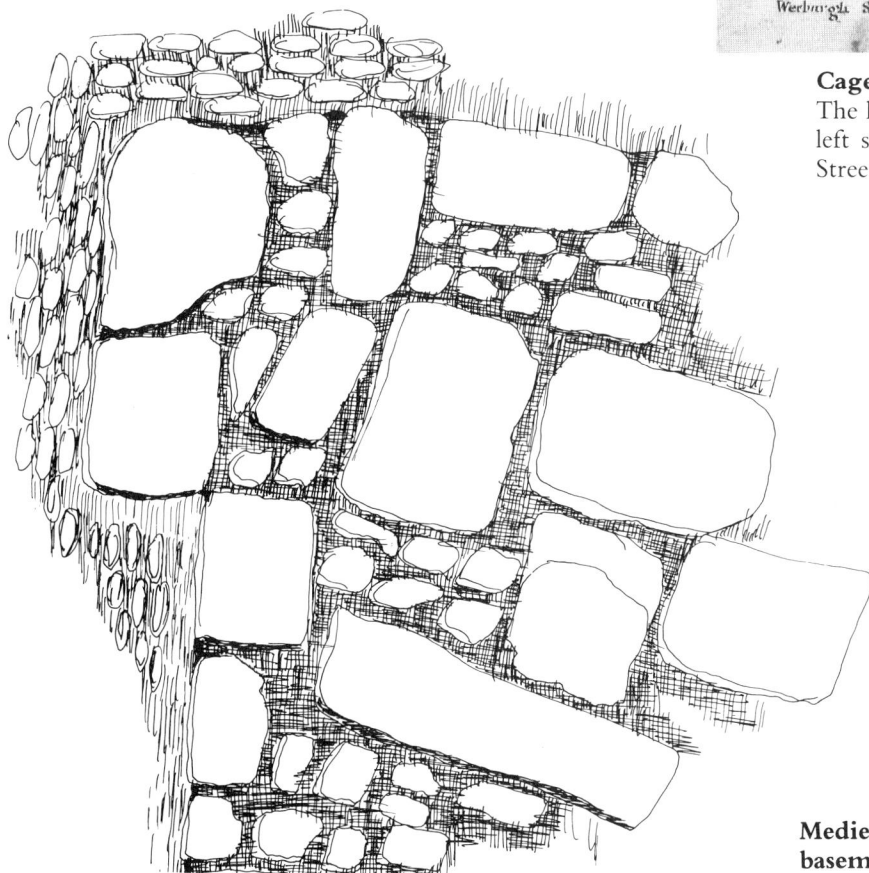

Medieval street and pavement flags from a basement in Temple Bar.

City Seal.

The City Seal is 13th century and is the earliest item in the City regalia. Showing the city under siege, two sentries on the central watch tower are sounding the alarm, two heralds on the walls are doing likewise, and on top of the gate towers, two archers are aiming their crossbows. The decapitated heads of three transgressors are impaled over the gate as a grisly warning. On the second bronze seal (not illustrated) — two moulds were used to make a double sided wax impression — the scene depicts the city at peace as signified by a merchant ship at sea. Stamped around the rim of both seals are the words "Sigillum Commune Civium Dubline" or "The Common Seal of the City of Dublin".

City Stocks.

Punishment for crime might place the hapless miscreant into the City Stocks where he was pelted with fruit (or worse, to the great danger of the eyes) or lambasted with insults. The stocks still survive today in the crypt of Christ Church Cathedral.

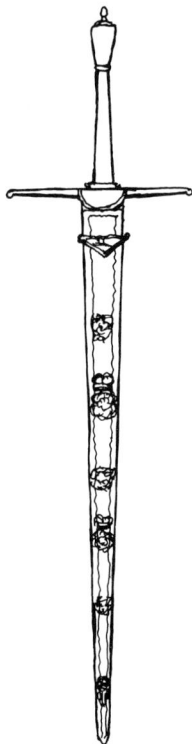

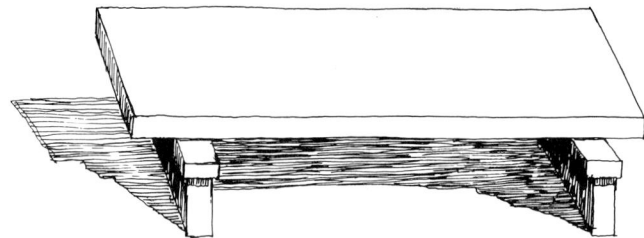

City Sword.

The City Sword is 14th century. It was carried before the Mayor when he travelled in public. Once a year the Mayor, Corporation and Guilds "rode the Franchises"; i.e. they ceremoniously rode around the boundaries of the city's limits.

The 1500's brought about some fundamental changes in the city. The Reformation arrived, de facto, in 1536 when King Henry VIII was officially appointed Head of the Church in Ireland. Almost all of the monasteries and abbeys were closed and their properties confiscated. Their loss went beyond their religious contribution as these institutions also provided many social services especially for the poor and the sick. Persecution of priests and catholics did take place in this period but it was a half-hearted attempt until a more determined and sustained process began in the 17th century. Nevertheless, a number of priests and bishops were hunted down. Archbishop Dermot O'Hurley of Cashel was imprisoned in Dublin Castle and later hanged in Hoggen Green in 1584.

In the rest of Ireland political turmoil and the last great attempts by the remaining Gaelic chieftains to assert independence led to many wars of attrition. Dublin was the key distribution centre for the English armies during their military campaigns and the port was never busier. A new wave of immigrants, mostly professionals of one sort or another including civil servants, accountants and skilled craftsmen, arrived from the mid 1500's.

The English authorities now decided to take a direct hand in ruling Ireland and no longer relied on the loyalties of the former ruling classes i.e. the direct descendants of the Anglo Norman lords. Some able but very ruthless Lords Deputy put their stamp on affairs and Dublin took shape as the undisputed capital (from an English point of view) of all Ireland.

A pair of graphic views depicting the retribution taken against rebels or those accused of treason against the English Crown.

Sir Henry Sidney departs Dublin

"These trunckles heddes do playnly showe each rebelles fatall end, and what a haynous crime it is, the Queene for to offend".

O Sydney worthy of tryple re-
nowne,
For plagyng the traytours that
troubled the crowne. 1581.

Sir Henry's Triumphant Return

Engravings from Images of Irelande by John Derricke 1581, give an idea of what medieval Dublin looked like. In the first picture the Lord Deputy, Sir Henry Sidney, sets out on a military expedition (note the heads of the rebels displayed on poles over the gates of Dublin Castle).

Chapter 3

BREAKING FREE

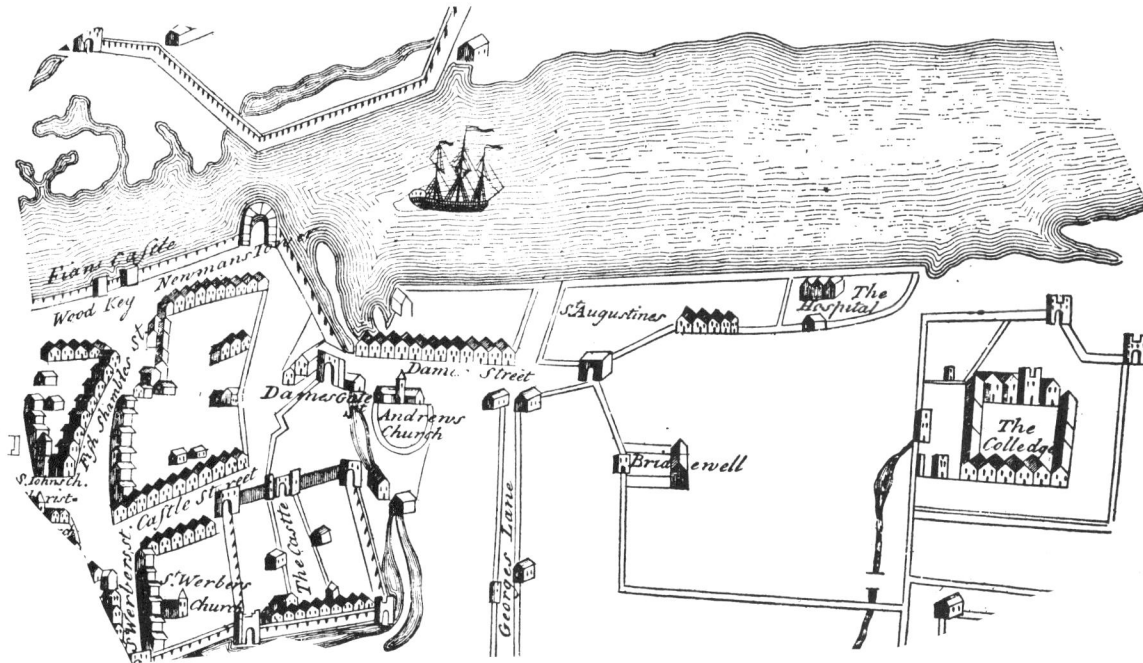

John Speed's Map 1610

This is Dublin's first known map of the complete city (only the part covering Temple Bar is shown here). Much of modern Temple Bar was still covered by the tidal waters of the Liffey.

There was a terrace of houses along one side of Dame Street near Dames' Gate. Only three secular buildings existed further East; Trinity College, Carey's Hospital (later Chichester House and ultimately Parliament House), and the Bridewell. The latter building was built around 1600 to house vagrants and unfortunates smitten with plague. The name Bridewell originates from a predecessor of this prison which was located near St. Brigid's Well.

Now a weakened and dispirited municipality, Dublin faced into the 17th century with uncertainty and apathy. But the forces that could influence the greatest growth in size and prestige that the city had ever experienced were starting to gather. The merchant and titled classes, who came over to Dublin from England in the late 1500's, wanted to expand beyond the stifling cocoon of the city walls. Their efforts resulted in an increase from a population of 18,000 citizens in 1600 to 40,000 in 1700 despite another plague in 1604 and a huge drop in numbers during the calamitous Cromwellian Wars of the 1650's. Even more striking was the physical enlargement of the town which increased fivefold over a hundred years. But this period of growth would have to wait until 1660.

John Speed's map of 1610 shows little new development yet outside the walls and almost none at all to the East. The authorities at this time were increasing their persecution of Catholics and this, more than civic improvements, seemed to absorb most of their attentions. An occasional notable new building came along such as the Earl of Cork's new mansion on Cork Hill (1600) or the resited Custom House beside present-day Grattan Bridge. Also, during his seven year term of office as Lord Deputy, Sir Thomas Wentworth effected some improvements on the fabric of the city.

Unfortunately, matters deteriorated seriously from 1642 on the outbreak of the English civil war. An abortive siege of Dublin by the native Irish in 1646 was followed by the loss of the royalist held city to the parliamentarians a year later. In 1649 Oliver Cromwell landed at Ringsend and his troops showed scant respect for the people and buildings of Dublin. Further, all Catholic landowners were to suffer transplantation and fortfeiture of property or even death. Caught between shifting loyalties and ruthless edicts, the hard-pressed people of Dublin could hardly be blamed for letting the town moulder away. There was, however, a light at the end of the tunnel.

In 1660, Charles II was crowned King of England and the Restoration Period ushered in a carefully planned expansion of the city.

A stone buttress from Copper Alley.
This structure was possibly built from stone salvaged from the old city walls, a common practice in years gone by.

Coins minted in Dublin from 1035 (Norse) to 1690 (King James II).

Hiberno-Norse   C 1035

James I
One shilling
1605

One shilling
Gun money
1690

King John penny
1204-1211

The new Lord Lieutenant, the Duke of Ormonde, had ambitious plans to turn Dublin into a beautiful and enriched city. New quays were constructed and buildings were started along Dame Street. In 1662, the Smock Alley Theatre was opened by John Ogilby and of great convenience to Northsiders attending plays here, the first Essex Bridge was built in 1676 by Sir Humphrey Jervis.

Huguenots started to arrive in their thousands into Dublin after the revocation of the Edict of Nantes in 1685 and their contribution to the life, business and building of Dublin was enormous. The front gabled house, the "Dutch Billy", was a product of these and later Dutch immigrants and was the most common form of house building in Dublin until the Georgian era.

Before the century was over there was, once more, political upheaval that threw the city into confusion. King James II arrived in Dublin in 1689, restored religious freedom to Catholics, established a Royal Mint in Capel Street and generally upset the status quo. Just as the populace accommodated themselves to the new liberalisations or restrictions (depending on your point of view), the whole system was turned topsy turvy when, a year later, a victorious William of Orange was welcomed by the relieved Protestants. New Penal Laws were enforced against the Catholics. Within another year and for the next century the Protestant ascendancy class in Dublin assumed the role of the main decision maker for the future of Dublin.

Lord Mayor's Chain of Office and Mace.

In 1665 Sir Daniel Bellingham, the first person to use the prefix "Lord" in front of Mayor, provided himself with a Great Mace which, with the City Sword, was to be carried before him on formal occasions. Made of silver gilt and measuring sixty and three quarter inches (1.5m) in length, the mace is identical in size to that of London.

The original Great Chain of Office was a gift from Charles II but it disappeared after the Battle of the Boyne. King William of Orange issued a replacement which is still being worn almost 300 years later. Each alternate link consists of a letter "S" standing for "Sovereign". Other links represent a harp, a portcullis, the Tudor Rose and the Trefoil-shaped Knot which is the floral device of Ireland. The large gold medal is stamped with the bust of William.

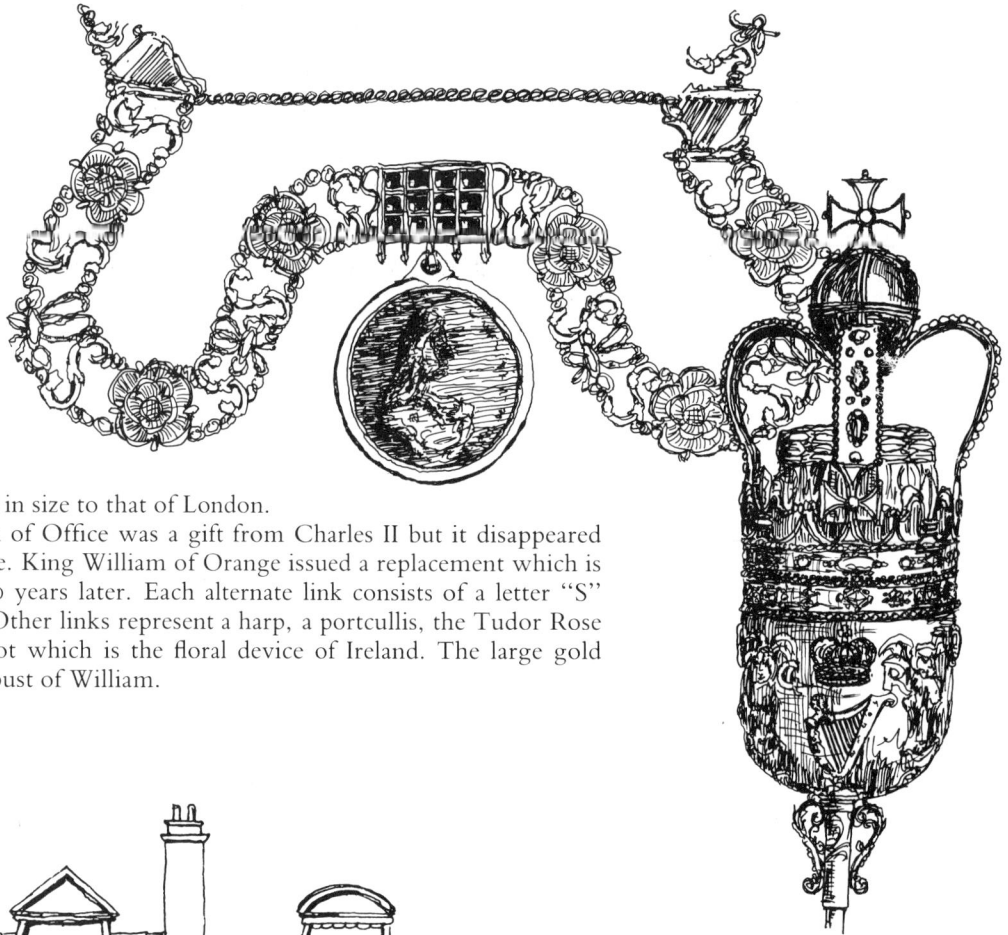

"Dutch Billy".

Example of a typical "Dutch Billy" front gabled house of c 1700. This house style spread out all over Dublin but was especially prominent in the Liberties (South and West of Dublin Castle) where the Huguenots mainly settled. Only a handful of examples survive today.

The mouth of the River Poddle

Before the new dockside at the Custom House Quay (now the West end of Wellington Quay) could be built (in 1620/21), an enormous amount of land reclamation had to be carried out. This coincided with the development of the quays on the North side. One objective of this was to have a narrower but deeper river to allow larger hulled ships to come up the river. This aim was never satisfactorily fulfilled which eventually led to shipping being docked further and further downriver as the centuries advanced.

In the meantime, the land reclamation directly afforded the opportunity to develop the area along present Essex and Fleet Streets. Previously subjected to high tide flooding the Liffey was now tamed. The Poddle was culverted and built over. Today it pours out into the Liffey through an archway under Wellington Quay, a little east of the Clarence Hotel. Humiliated now and hidden from view within the city limits, this is a sad exit for a river that was the lifeblood of the city for eight hundred years.

The iron grating across the arch was placed there after the abortive 1867 Fenian Rising to prevent insurgents, armed with explosives, from gaining entrance to the culvert which runs directly past Dublin Castle.

TEMPLE BAR c 1760s

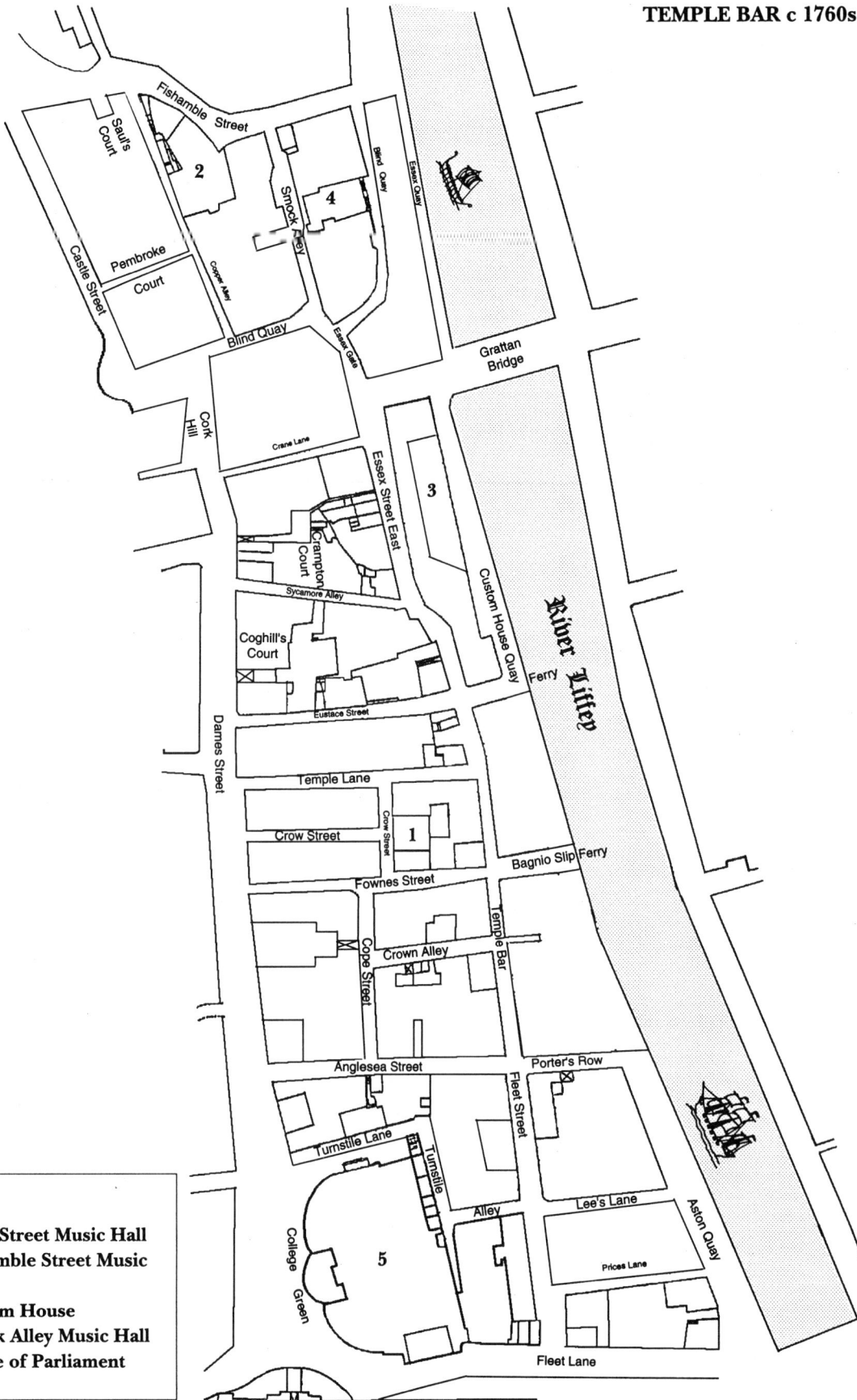

Fishamble Street

Saul's Court

2

Blind Quay

Essex Quay

Smock Alley

4

Castle Street

Pembroke Court

Copper Alley

Blind Quay

Essex Gate

Grattan Bridge

Cork Hill

Crane Lane

Essex Street East

3

Custom House Quay

River Liffey

Crampton Court

Sycamore Alley

Coghill's Court

Ferry

Eustace Street

Dames Street

Temple Lane

Crow Street

Crow Street

1

Bagnio Slip Ferry

Fownes Street

Cope Street

Crown Alley

Temple Bar

Anglesea Street

Porter's Row

Fleet Street

Turnstile Lane

Turnstile Alley

Lee's Lane

Aston Quay

College Green

5

Prices Lane

Fleet Lane

KEY
1 Crow Street Music Hall
2 Fishamble Street Music Hall
3 Custom House
4 Smock Alley Music Hall
5 House of Parliament

THE EIGHTEENTH CENTURY

This was the century when Temple Bar took on the shape most familiar to us today. The Georgian style of house replaced its predecessors to such an extent that virtually nothing remains now above ground from before this time.

Part of the charm of Temple Bar now results from the fact that the main eighteenth century residential squares and avenues were planned away from this district and this left intact the system of short, narrow and sometimes winding streets. This did not mean the absence of some very fine Georgian mansions with highly decorative interiors. Most of these residences were subsequently turned into offices and warehouses and former features became hidden or damaged.

The periphery of Temple Bar did benefit from the work of the Wide Street Commissioners (see page 36) when they opened Parliament Street, Westmoreland Street and Wellington Quay and widened Dame Street.

Life in Temple Bar was a very concentrated affair and many trades and professions which settled here served the whole city. Three of the city's most important entertainment venues were within the borders; the Music Hall in Fishamble Street and the Crow Street and Smock Alley Theatres.

The streets witnessed their fair share of high fashion both from their own residents and from those thronging to the theatres, state occasions in Dublin Castle or the sittings of the Parliament House. Taverns and coffee houses did a thriving business and the shops sold everything from wigs to sails for ships.

Parliament House (started 1728) was the single most important architectural achievement in the first half of the 18th century not only in Temple Bar but in the whole country. A wealthy colonial ascendancy were determined to show their peers in London and elsewhere that Dublin was at the forefront of business, the arts and sophistication.

While the fruits of commerce and the finer things of life were amply availed of by the privileged classes the situation of the poor masses (usually Catholics) was difficult if not intolerable. Denied political and religious rights and entry to many professions and trades, this underclass would have to wait until the next century for any legal relief.

THE OLD CUSTOM HOUSE

This scene reveals a wealth of information on the Dublin of the day (1753). In the first place the Custom House itself, a commodious building by the standards of the 18th century, was the city's first major office block. Replacing an earlier building further up the river at Merchants' Quay, it was built in 1707.

Evidence that only four small ships could be berthed at the same time is clear from the print. Larger ships unloaded downriver into lighters and barges, several of which can be seen in the picture.

Building is dense along this stretch of the Liffey and the skyline is punctuated by the tower of Christ Church and in the far distance the spire of the Royal Hospital, Kilmainham. A statue of George I stands on Essex Bridge. The bridge in this view was replaced by a new structure shortly after this engraving was made. Note that Parliament Street has not yet been opened.

On the north side of the river a carriage and two drays (one possibly carrying wine or porter or even water) move along a very rutted road. Two men are fishing, more from necessity than for sport.

When the new Custom House was opened in 1791 this old building was converted for a while into a military barracks.

MUSIC HALL, FISHAMBLE STREET 1785

Handel had already written the score of the "Messiah" two months earlier when he sailed to Dublin in November 1741. His reputation in London had suffered a setback and he looked forward to a more appreciative audience in the Irish capital. He was not to be disappointed.

Several performances of some of his earlier works were given, for charitable foundations around Christmas and the New Year, and were received with delight by Dublin audiences. In March 1742 it was revealed that his new oratorio "Messiah" would get its first public hearing in William Neal's one year old Music Hall in Fishamble Street.

Designed by architect Richard Cassels, the hall was a perfect venue and was described by Handel as one of the best he had seen anywhere. On Tuesday 13th April, 1742, over seven hundred men (without their swords) and women (without their hoops) packed in to hear the solo singers, twenty players and the cathedral choirs of St. Patrick's and Christ Church render one of the most sublime pieces of music ever composed. The performance was an outstanding success and it encouraged Handel over the earlier trough in his career.

Neal's Music Hall continued to offer first rate shows until a gradual fall off in business after the Act of Union forced the owners to sell. Shows from pantomime to Shakespeare were produced and the hall was renamed "The Sans Pareil Theatre" and then the "Prince of Wales" until Kennan & Sons, an iron works, took it over in 1868.

FISHAMBLE STREET. DUBLIN. 1797.

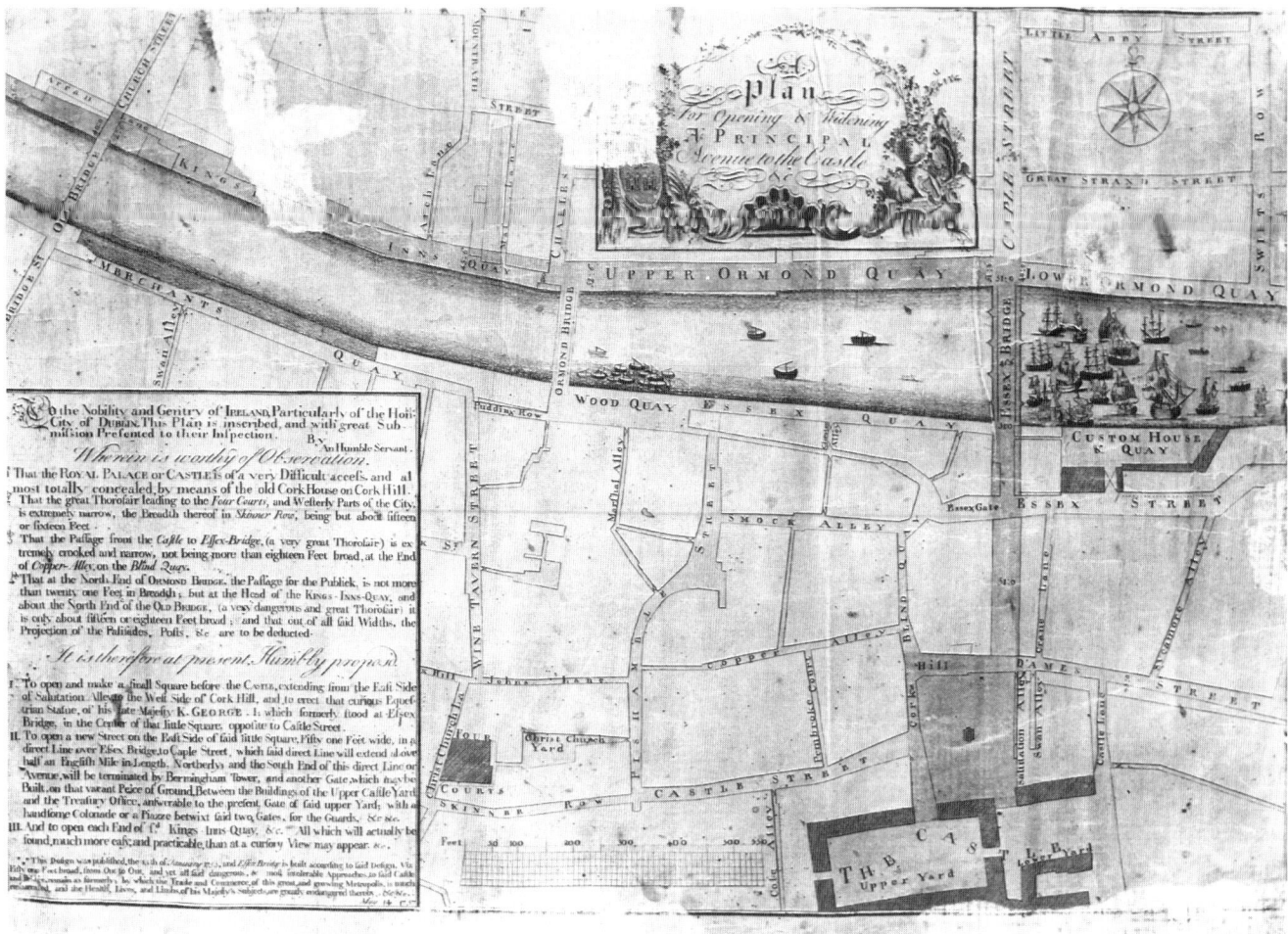

Parliament Street and the Wide Streets Commissioners (1758-1851)

Traffic congestion is not a new phenomenon. In 1749 a parliamentary committee examined the bottleneck caused at Essex Bridge for traffic approaching the Castle, the Custom House and Parliament House itself (see 1750's map). It was resolved in 1758 to build a direct route from the bridge to the Castle and to this end £7,000 was allocated for the work and twenty one commissioners appointed to oversee the task.

Originally the street was going to be called Fortescue Street but Alderman Philip Crampton, who owned most of the land involved, proposed that the street be named Parliament Street.

Completed in 1762 the wide new avenue was appreciated by everyone except those tenants (the owners had been compensated) who lost their homes literally overnight. As recounted at the time, "they unroofed the houses in the middle of the night to get people out for street widening".

Following the successful creation of Parliament Street, the Commissioners, over the next ninety three years, went on to build or widen Dame Street, Foster Place, Wellington Quay, Westmoreland Street, Sackville (O'Connell) Street and many others. The Commissioners also concerned themselves with the front elevations of the buildings along these streets and their work left a heritage of very elegant thoroughfares.

36

James Malton's famous view of College Green 1793

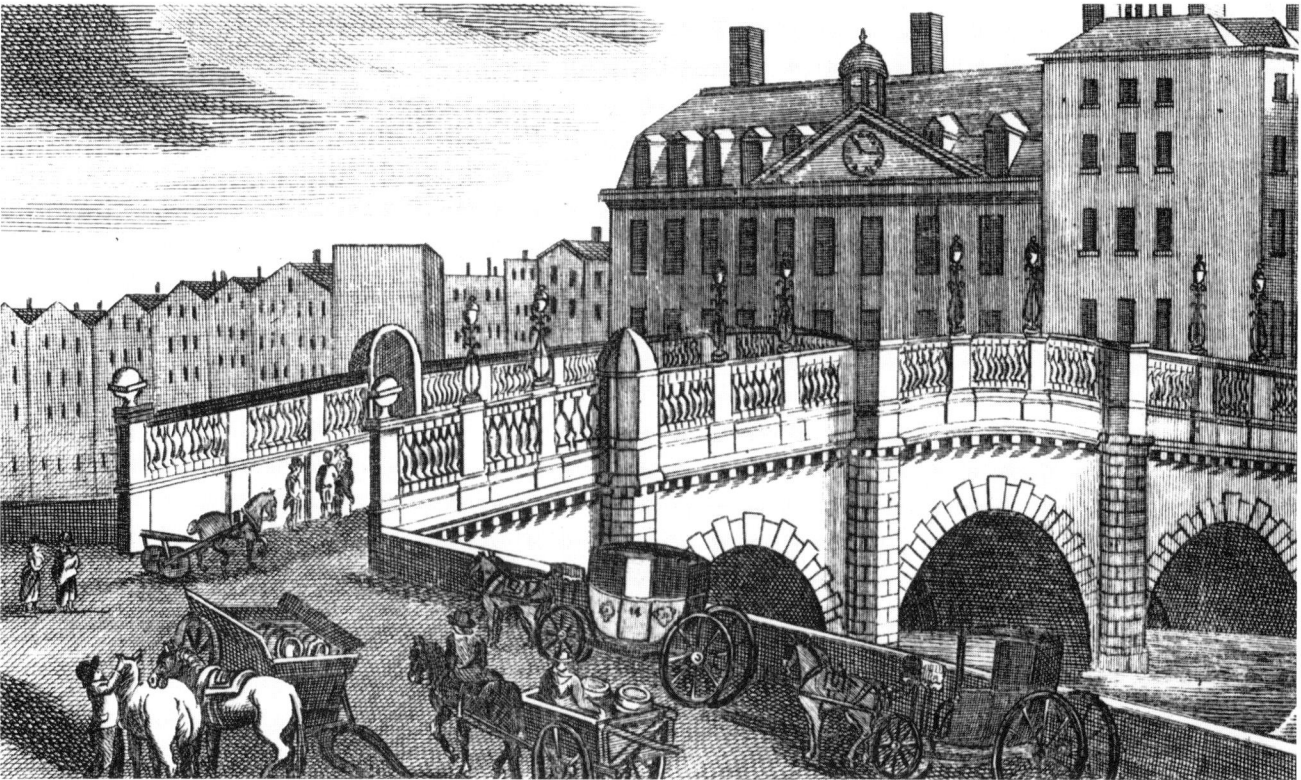

Old Essex Bridge.
Late 18th century view across Essex Bridge of the newly opened Parliament Street and the redundant (since 1791) Custom House. Wellington Quay is not yet built and the houses are standing right onto the river. This picture compares interestingly with the earlier view (1753) on page 34.

Georgian Doorway with stone surround, Fownes Street.

Georgian Door Knocker, Foster Place.

A view towards Dame Street in 1753.

The "Dutch Billy" gabled houses have not yet been replaced by the Georgian houses which followed the reconstruction of the street by the Wide Streets Commissioners in 1769. The obelisks stand in front of Trinity College.

An intractable insurance problem emerged in 1700 when a missing galley, the "Ouzel", returned after five years by which stage, of course, the insurance money had been paid out. Satisfactory arbitration solved the difficulty and also led to the founding of the Ouzel Galley Society which was later to become the Dublin Chamber of Commerce (1783).

The building onto which the plaque is affixed is a replica of the old Commercial Buildings (erected 1799 on a small court called Fownes Court) which now faces west instead of south as before.

Sign of the Ouzel Galley Society, Dame Street.

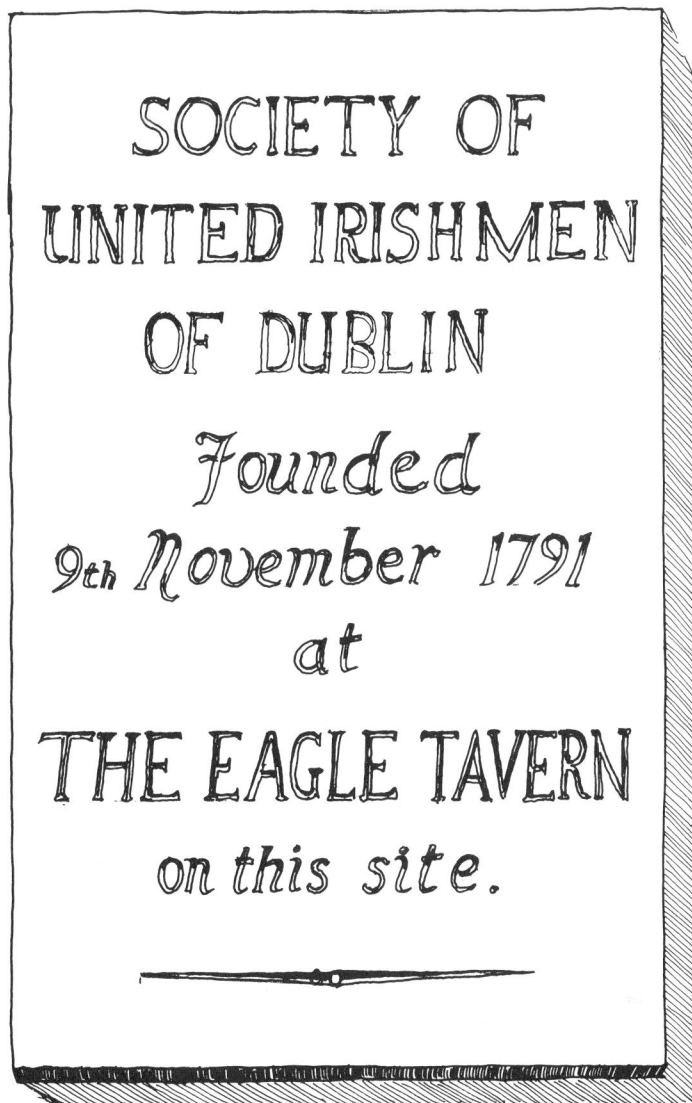

Plaque to The Eagle Tavern, 4/5 Eustace Street.

This was one of the most famous taverns in the whole city. Built around 1712 it was frequented by many groups, guilds, clubs and sometimes very opposing organisations. The meetings of the Dublin Volunteers (a Protestant Ascendancy Group) took place here in 1782 and in 1791 the first clandestine meeting of the United Irishmen of Dublin was held in the Eagle. More innocuous were the assemblies of the Guild of Cooks, a public spirited society known as the "Whigs of the Capital", the Grand Masters Lodge of the Irish Free Masons and a county Kerry Association of Gentlemen. All grist to the tavern's mill as meetings can be very thirsty affairs.

Last glasses in the "Eagle" were emptied around 1812 and three years later the Quakers bought the property.

TEMPLE BAR c 1820s

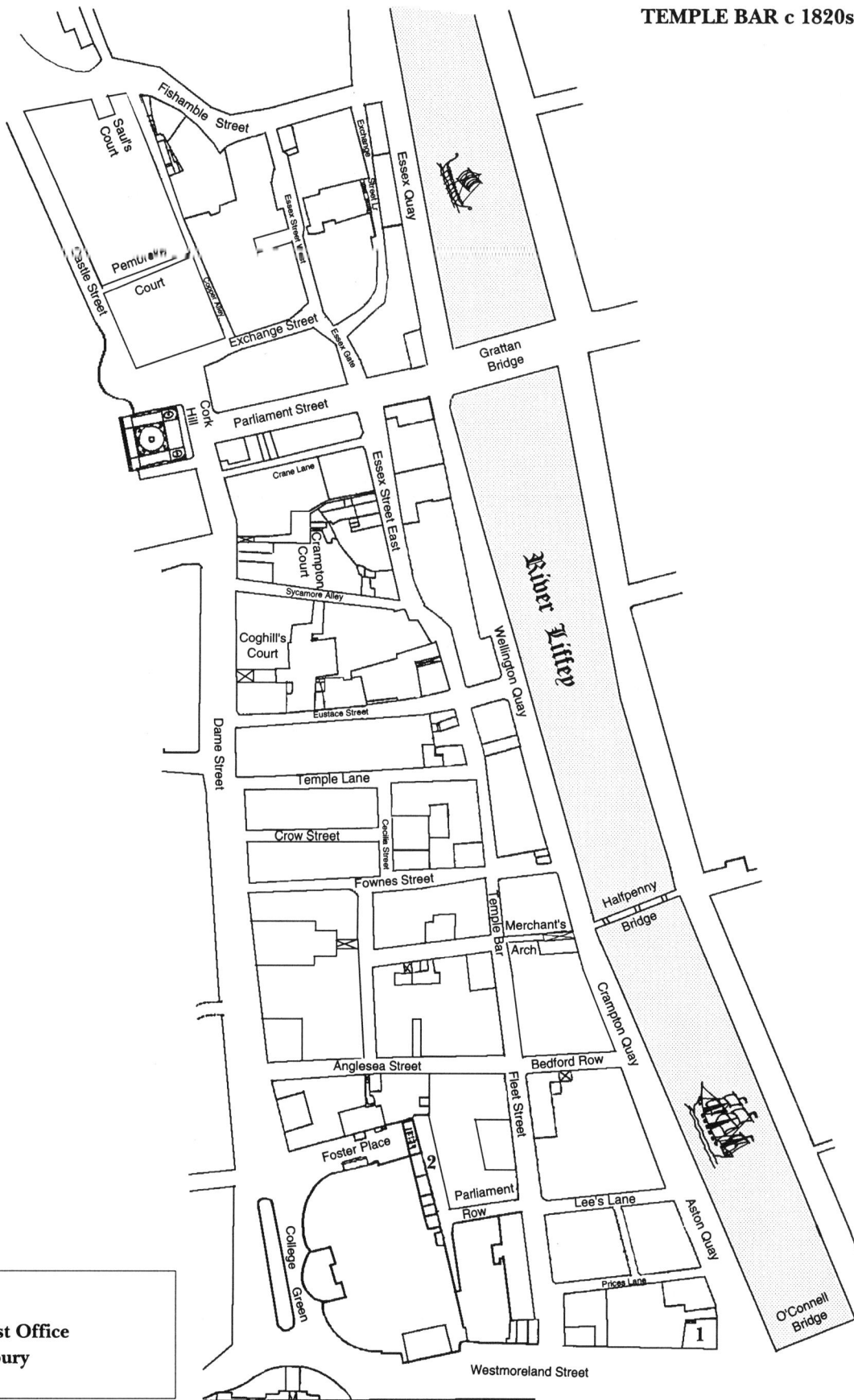

Saul's Court

Fishamble Street

Exchange Street

Essex Quay

Castle Street

Pembroke Court

Essex Street West

Essex Gate

Exchange Street

Grattan Bridge

Cork Hill

Parliament Street

Crane Lane

Essex Street East

Crampton Court

Sycamore Alley

River Liffey

Coghill's Court

Eustace Street

Wellington Quay

Dame Street

Temple Lane

Crow Street

Cecilia Street

Fownes Street

Halfpenny Bridge

Temple Bar

Merchant's Arch

Crampton Quay

Anglesea Street

Bedford Row

Foster Place

Fleet Street

2

Parliament Row

Lee's Lane

Aston Quay

College Green

Prices Lane

1

O'Connell Bridge

Westmoreland Street

KEY
1 Ballast Office
2 Armoury

40

Chapter 4

OBEDIENTIA CIVIUM URBIS FELICITAS

Coat-of-Arms in the pediment of the Bank of Ireland, College Green.

THE NINETEENTH CENTURY

It was more a change of use than any physical alteration in the street patterns that marked out the nineteenth century. There was less of a residential (except for tenement living) and more of a commercial content in the street life. While shipping had moved further downriver Temple Bar's warehouses were still in great demand.

In the latter half of the century Dame Street, College Green and Westmoreland Street took on a decidedly business air with banks and insurance companies building magnificent new Victorian edifaces.

There were a number of physical obstructions on the streets or quays which impeded smooth movement of traffic. These were eliminated by the construction of Wellington Quay and Lord Edward Street.

Bank of Ireland Sentry Box and Cannon.

These are reminders that the bank had its own guard of soldiers throughout the 19th century and up to the middle of this century. There was even an associated pageantry for the ceremonial changing of the guard. This agreeable custom was dispensed with on the outbreak of the Second World War.

Bank of Ireland Yeomanry 1813.

Raised in 1797 and disbanded in the early 1820's. The illustration shows a captain based on a painting by Robert Gibbs in the Civic Museum. In other organisations similar Yeomanry were formed to afford protection from rabble and rebels.

(Courtesy Glenn Thompson).

Bank of Ireland Cash Office.

The Cash Office was built in 1804 when the House of Commons was converted for bank use. It was designed by Francis Johnston.

College Green into Dame Street

Westmoreland Street c 1820

City of Dublin Workingmen's Club.

Well over a hundred years old this club started life in one of the buildings huddled up close to Christ Church Cathedral. When those houses were cleared around 1886 to give open space around the church, the club bought the premises on Wellington Quay (1888) with the compensation money. Note the old Irish lettering on the facia board.

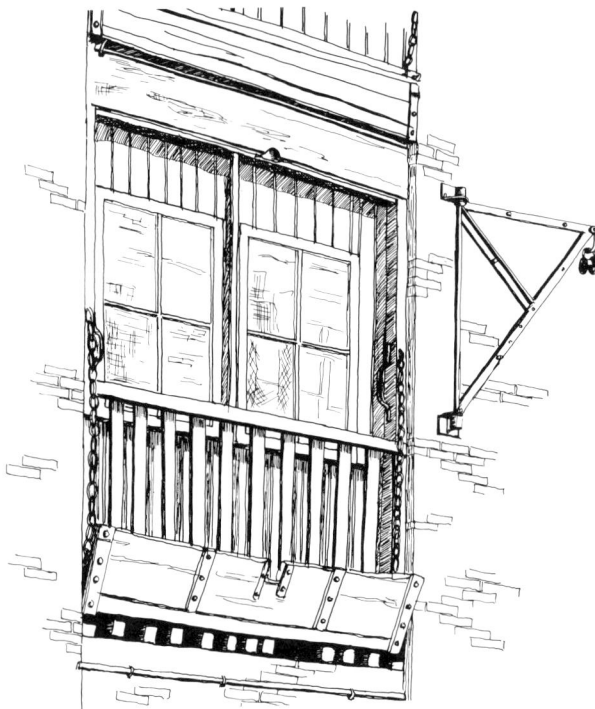

Several examples of upper storey loading bays still exist in this area of Temple Bar indicating the presence of many 19th century warehouses.

Loading Bay, Temple Lane.

44

Dublin City's Coat of Arms

Lamp standards, Temple Bar.

The Coat of Arms was first granted officially to Dublin Corporation in 1607 by Daniel Molyneux, Ulster King of Arms and Principal Herald of all Ireland.

Derived from a more ancient device (see City Seal page 24) the flames leaping from the three castles symbolise, not the city burning, rather the zeal of the citizens to defend their city.

"Obedientia Civicum Urbis Felicitas" roughly translates as "Obedient Citizens make a Happy City".

Coal Covers

(along many pavements in Temple Bar)

Most Georgian houses were built over a cellar which contained the kitchen, scullery, a housemaid's bedroom (many cellars had windows) and storerooms. Coal was lowered into the cellar through the simple but expedient method of using a hole in the pavement. The holes were covered by iron lids which had varied and attractive designs on their faces. Even though many generations of feet have been wearing them away since, their designs can still be appreciated especially on quieter streets.

Footscraper

(Merchants' Hall).

There seem to be as many designs of footscrapers as there were Georgian houses. But the individuality within a prescribed frame-work was a hall-mark of 18th century house-building.

45

All the street surfaces in this part of Dublin in the last century were composed of stone setts which were very hard wearing. By the 1980's only a handful of streets in Temple Bar still retained their setts but since then, in an ongoing programme, many streets have been relaid with setts.

Obviously there is a particular skill needed to lay them and some fine possibilities for intricate designs emerge at junctions as this illustration shows.

In the days of iron clad horse hooves and cart wheels the din over the stone setts was most disturbing. To alleviate the stress caused to sick people in rooms overlooking the streets, straw was placed over the surface leading to and from the house to soften the racket.

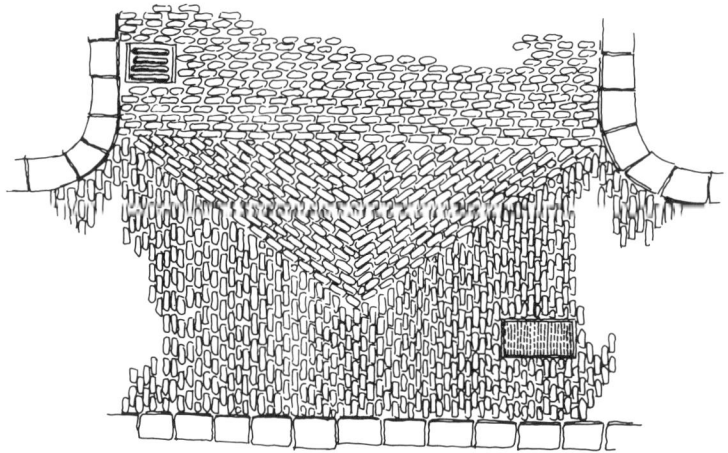

Street Setts

Bollard, Foster Place.
Bollards, either granite or iron, were erected to protect pillars
or gateways from the wheels of carts.

Fitzgeralds, Westmoreland Street.
Another reminder of a previous
owner and usage.

46

The Vestment Warehouse, Parliament Street.
Miss Catherine Cahill's was a leading house (1860 to 1920's) for all forms of church vestments, altar linens, banners and clerical garb.

Former McBirney's Stores, now Virgin Megastore, Aston Quay.
This feature of the erstwhile owners was left in place when the new occupants took over in the 1980's.

Old Dolphin Hotel and Michael Nugent's, Essex Street East.
Carved lettering from the two premises built by the same family.

Relief from Shamrock Chambers, Eustace Street.
This used to be the headquarters of Lipton's Tea & Provisions Merchants, once a household name in Dublin.

Head Carving, Eustace Street.
In the nineteenth century many firms advertised either their business or their importance by commissioning small classical decorations over their ground floor facades.

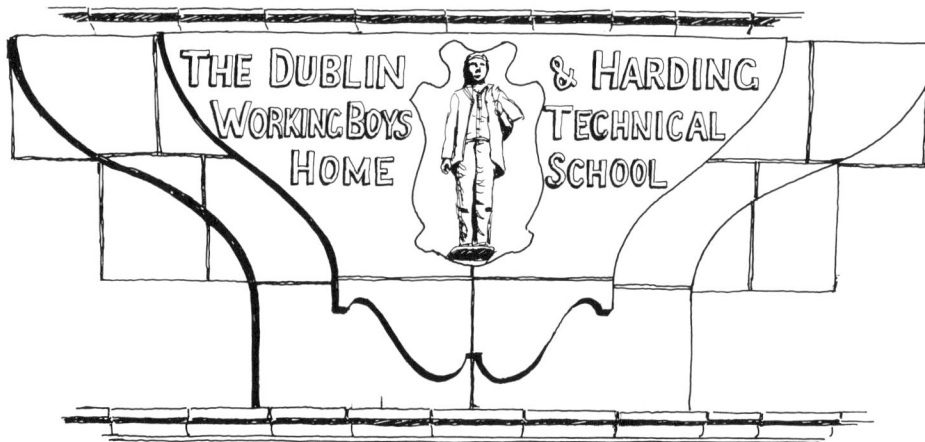

THE DUBLIN & HARDING
WORKING BOYS TECHNICAL
HOME SCHOOL

Harding Boys Home, Lord Edward Street.
School and home for teen-age boy apprentices, founded in 1876.

The Bell of Michael and John's Church, Essex Street West.
In 1818 this historic bell was the first to ring out from a Catholic church in Dublin since the Reformation took effect in 1537.

Original clock of the former Yorkshire Insurance Company, College Green.
Until the Fire Brigade was formed in 1862 insurance companies provided a fire fighting service but usually only to their own clients. The clock is coloured red, a colour introduced by the insurance companies and now internationally used by fire brigades.

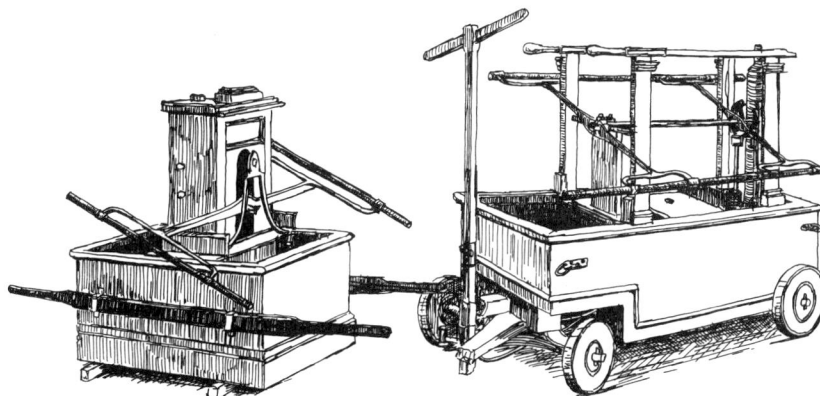

Water Pumps, St. Werburgh's Church.
These preserved pumps are a relic of the 18th century when fires were attended to by volunteers organised from parish churches.

49

Halfpenny Bridge mid 1820's

This is a most striking view along the newly constructed Wellington Quay. While the road surface leaves something to be desired, the pathway and wall along the river have obviously become a popular promenade. This is not surprising as the building of Wellington Quay in 1816 opened up an entirely new vista along the quays.

The buildings on the left are brand new and no unsightly gaps are evident along the quays. Two boxes, one at each end, are standing on the Halfpenny Bridge to provide shelter for the toll collectors who also had to prevent horsemen from using the bridge.

The view shows a leisurely pace of life and the impression given is of a well-to-do city. This is misleading as many of the houses on the right were little more than overcrowded tenements. Also the city could be a very smoggy place as evidenced by the smoke coming from nearly every chimney.

Daly's Club 18th Century

Patrick Daly's Club started modestly enough in a coffee house but within a few years Francis Johnston received his first Dublin commission to design a new granite faced building on College Green stretching from Anglesea Street to Foster Place. It opened in 1789. A footpath across Foster Place and a private underground passage to the Parliament House was provided to members. The result was a sumptuous palace which catered very well and discreetly for rich bucks and the honourable Members of Parliament.

Stories of round-the-clock gambling, estates wagered or drunk away, parliamentary differences compromised and bitter quarrels settled by duels were the norm at Daly's. The poor were scandalised and the gentry occasionally embarrassed.

The level and quality of the business dropped off after the Act of Union in 1800. Daly's struggled on for a while as if trying to ignore the profound political and social changes taking place outside. However, it had to finally capitulate and the doors were closed for good in 1823.

Daly's Club Today

The building has since passed through a succession of tenants including insurance companies and stockbrokers. The wing buildings at each end have been removed for redevelopment and two extra storeys have been added on.

Thomas Read & Co., Parliament Street

James Read opened his knife and sword making shop and forge in 1670 on Blind Quay (Lower Exchange Street). His sister Elizabeth married a Richard Guinness whose son Arthur went on to found one of the world's greatest brewing firms.

James died in 1744 and the business passed to his nephew John who previously had been elected warden of the Guild of Cutlers. John acquired, in 1750, a property in what was then the busy little street of Crane Lane, the direct route from Dame Street to the docks and Custom House Quay. He lived over the shop and was on hand to see a new opportunity presenting itself. Parliament Street was being laid out in the late 1750's and he bought a plot to the rear of his Crane Lane premises and reversed his accommodation using the Parliament Street side for his shop entrance.

The new shop prospered and Read's manufactured halberds, swords, daggers, knives and surgical aids.

When John died in 1776 he left the concern to his son Thomas after whom the business is currently named. In 1988, Mr Jack Cowle, the last member of the Read family, retired and for the first time in over two hundred years the firm passed to a different but nonetheless committed family, the Butlers.

There are many examples on display in the preserved old cases and shelves of the sharp ends of the business including Read-made old swords, butchers' knives, catering knives, ivory handled knives, scalpels, reputedly the world's smallest scissors and the world's largest penknife containing five hundred and seventy six blades. The basement still contains the original forge used by John Read.

Thomas Read & Co., Parliament Street

House of Lords

The barrel-vaulted chamber remains today much as it was when designed by Sir Edward Lovett Pearce in 1728. The reconstruction demanded by the authorities after the Act of Union in 1800 to remove all traces of the old Parliament was ignored by the Bank of Ireland in relation to this room. Thus was preserved intact one of the world's most unique examples of an 18th century legislature.

Most notable of the furnishings are the pair of tapestries thought to have been the design of Johann van der Hagen and woven (at 26 stitches to the inch/2.5 cm) by John van Beaver, both Dutch craftsmen living in Dublin. Hung in 1733 the scenes depict "The Glorious Battle of the Boyne" and "The Glorious Defence of Londonderry". While the colours have faded somewhat their present condition is excellent.

The original carved oak mantlepiece is still in position. Made up of 1,233 separate pieces, the great chandelier dates from 1788 and was probably made at Chebsey's Glass Works near Ballybough Bridge in Dublin.

After the dissolution of Parliament one item did have a curious new usage. The Division Bell of the House of Commons was eventually sold to the Theatre Royal, Hawkins Street, as the call-bell and in later years the Gaiety Theatre used it to summon the staff together for payment of wages.

The Mace of the House of Commons.

The mace was made in England in 1765 for £244.4s.11 1/2d. It is 58 inches (147 cms) long and weighs 295 ounces (8.3 kgs). After the Act of Union, Speaker of the House, John Foster insisted that it remain in his custody until it was demanded back by a reconvened Parliament.

It was subsequently bought from his descendants by a London firm and purchased back again at a sale in Christie's in 1937 by the Bank of Ireland. The Mace of the House of Lords is in the National Museum.

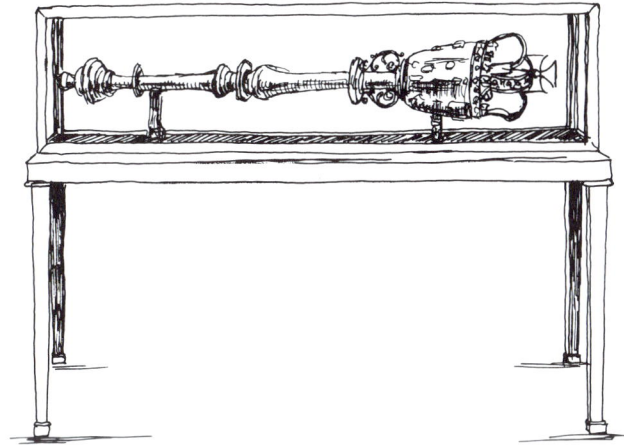

Alan McShane Ltd.

Alan McShane Ltd. is a long established family run office equipment business. It now occupies Fownes Street Buildings (at the corner of Temple Bar), a nicely crafted red brick building once the offices, warehouses and stables of William Hogg & Co., Wine Importers. One or two of the dray horses names are still in their slots on the wall of the old stables at the rear of the premises, now turned into a car park. The thick walls of McShanes and the dry, ambient atmosphere of the old cellars offer ideal conditions for the storage of paper products.

55

Olympia Theatre

One of the most colourful and boisterous nights in the history of the Irish theatre was that which marked the opening of Dan Lowry's Star of Erin Music Hall on Monday 22nd December 1879 on Crampton Court. There was standing room only. Trinity students came in force (entrance was cheap) and rapid deployment of soldiers was necessary. Admission was; gallery 1s., stalls 6d., reserved seats 1/6d.

The curtain rose at 8 pm. Also present was Dan Lowry's son (he had taken a break from running the family's other two theatres in Liverpool), his grandson — a talented musician — conducted the orchestra, and another grandson was billed as a comedian. Truly a Lowry affair.

Quickfire variety, song and dance (from Little Nelly), a contortionist, a trapeze artist cum weightlifter and a Punch and Judy show rounded off the performance.

In 1817 the theatre was reconstructed and the entrance in Dame Street, with its beautiful and characteristic canopy, was added. The old music hall was renamed the "Empire Theatre of Varieties".

With the emergence of the Empire, plays, revues and pantomime were added to the original diet of musical variety. In due course the name changed to the "Olympia". In 1932, the comedian Jimmy O'Dea arrived and stayed until the start of the Second World War, at which point he moved to the "Gaiety". Jack Cruise had his first major success here in October, 1944. International stars to appear down the years included: Charlie Chaplin, Laurel and Hardy, Tyrone Power, Sybil Thorndyke, Margaret Rutherford and Margaret Lockwood.

In 1915, Peadar Kearney, the composer of the Irish National Anthem, turned the fire hoses on the orchestra and washed them out of the pit for playing the British Anthem. It was never played in the theatre again.

The Olympia suffered a near disaster in 1972 when, during rehearsals for "West Side Story", part of the building collapsed over the stage. Thankfully, no one was injured. The Corporation and the people of Dublin rallied to support the theatre and after the necessary repairs and some refurbishments were carried out, the doors were opened again.

Today, the theatre with its elegant old world interior is an essential ingredient in the capital's entertainment spectrum.

The Olympia Theatre, Dame Street.

**Allied Irish Banks,
Foster Place.**

Sir Thomas Lighton founded a bank in 1797 in partnership with Thomas Needham and Robert Shaw. In 1799 the bank bought new premises at No.4 Foster Place and expanded into No.5 in 1832. Lighton died in 1805, after which the bank became known as Shaw's. The Royal Bank bought Shaw's in 1836 and rebuilt the present edifice in 1859.

In 1966 the Royal Bank merged with the Provincial Bank of Ireland and the Munster and Leinster to form Allied Irish Banks plc.

The Foster Place branch is considered to be the oldest continuously operating bank in Dublin if not in the whole of Ireland.

Architect was Charles Geoghegan, the builder was Crowe & Sons and ironwork was by Courtney & Stephens.

The magnificent interior was equally matched by sensible advanced construction techniques. "The Dublin Builder" commented "The basement is entirely fireproof — all buildings of this class might in prudence be equally so".

The central span of the lantern roof is supported on twelve ornamented circular iron columns. The public area of the Cash Office is furnished with two large polished green Connemara marble fireplaces. Counters and seats are made of Cuban mahogany.

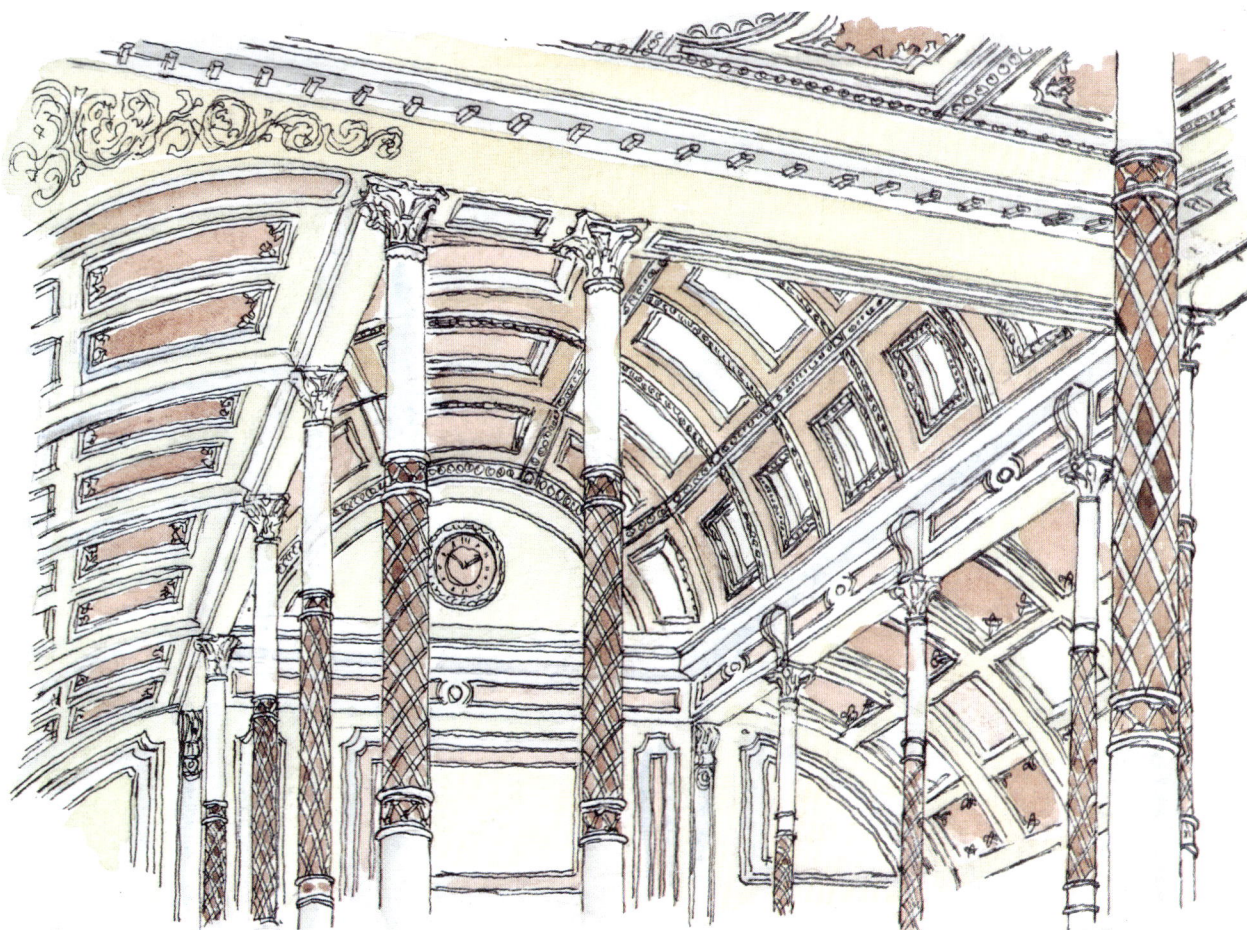

**Cash Office, Allied Irish Banks,
Foster Place.**

The Palace Bar, Fleet Street.

The Palace Bar retains a wonderful old-world Victorian atmosphere.

The street directories show that before "The Palace" it was Murray & Co., Grocers, Wine, Tea and Spirit Merchants (1917), James Hall, (1880) and John Sandford (1846), carried on in the same trade, showing a remarkable display of consistency. It has been owned by the Ahern family since 1945.

Perhaps one of Dublin's finest examples of a wooden shopfront which extends to the upper storeys belongs to No. 10 Anglesea Street, the property of the firm of James Flynn & Co. Solicitors. Originally built in 1898 for stockbrokers Waldron, Laurence, Ambrose & Co., it won the first Dublin Corporation Cultural Environment Award in 1981 for sensitive restoration, (it was at that time owned by Dillon & Waldron, stockbrokers).

James Flynn & Co.

4 to 7 Westmoreland Street

These buildings of varying styles successfully sit together side-by-side.

Quoting from the "Irish Builder" of 1870 the building on the left was "on the site formerly occupied by Mr. Marcus Moses (Music Warehouse). The front is a mixed style of architecture — Italian & Gothic — with modifications to suit our variable climate. Messrs. Cramer & Co. have opened a communication with a portion of the buildings that was formerly the Agricultural Bank in Fleet Street and the entire concern is now one of the largest music warehouses in the Kingdom." The architect was Mr. William G. Murray.

Again, for the building on the right, quoting from the "Irish Builder" of 1887. "Number 7 has been built of County Dublin granite and Portland stone. The foundation depth of fourteen feet was necessary because of peaty soil. The principal office (for the Northern Assurance Company) has a carved ceiling with woodwork being pitch-pine and mahogany". The architect was G.C. Ashlin.

This was Dublin's first purpose-built Telephone Exchange. Designed by the architectural firm of Sir Thomas Deane & Son, the building was completed in 1898 and was opened two years later by the National Telephone Company. The switchboard, which was very modern for its day, had a capacity for 1,600 lines and could handle up to 12,000 calls daily although the quality was not always satisfactory and all connections had to be made manually.

The hard pressed operators had more than frustrated callers to contend with as the Dublin Corporation minutes of 1914 reveal. They report a request received from the Post Office (it took over the operation in 1912) to lay wood block paving on Temple Bar and Crown Alley. Apparently the operators were having difficulty in hearing over the din of iron-shod horses and wheels on the stone setts outside.

Plans for the Rising in 1916 included the seizure of the Exchange but to the cost of the rebels they aborted the effort fearing the guard inside would be too strong. In the event there were no British Army soldiers present at all and the exchange provided valuable communication links for the authorities.

The building is still used as an automatic telephone exchange.

Telephone Exchange, Crown Alley.

The Central Bank, Dame Street.

For some years after the Constitution of the Irish Free State came into operation on December 6th 1922, British currency notes continued in general circulation. A change immediately to Irish currency would probably have lacked public support and confidence. By 1927, however, the Currency Commission had been established and within a year Irish notes and coinage came into being.

The Central Bank Act of 1942 replaced the Currency Commission with the present arrangement and successive legislation has strengthened and consolidated the role of the Central Bank.

The Associated Banks (Allied Irish, Bank of Ireland, etc.) require a bank themselves in which to transact business with each other and the Central Bank fulfills this function. Like any other institution the Government needs a banker and lodged in the Central Bank are the Exchequer revenues and the accounts of most of the individual Departments. Traditionally (although it is not required by statute) the majority of Central Bank Governors have been former Secretaries of the Department of Finance.

Housed in the old armoury of the Bank of Ireland in Foster Place since 1928, the Central Bank in 1965 (which was by now scattered in various offices around the city) commissioned Stephenson Gibney and Associates to design a new headquarters in Dame Street.

Work started on this controversial building in 1972 and was completed six years later. The floors were each jacked up from ground level, where they were constructed, and suspended from cantilevered trusses. This method of construction was the first of its kind in Ireland.

The Rock Garden and Oman's furniture removal warehouse, Crown Alley.

In this neighbourhood of converted warehouses Oman's is especially successful. Many features of the original building have been retained.

Sign over former Oman's Warehouse, Crown Alley.

Handwritten signs, explaining in verbose language the services on offer, were once a very agreeable form of facade decoration.

The art of signwriting (without so much quaint verbiage) is making a welcome comeback.

The Halfpenny Bridge.

Alternately called the Wellington Bridge (its first name), the Metal Bridge and the Liffey Bridge, it is popularly called the Halfpenny Bridge because of the toll once exacted to cross it.

William Walsh was the owner of seven reputedly leaky ferries and faced with a demand by the Corporation to repair them he made a decision. Business was falling anyway so he sought instead to build a pedestrian bridge. He was certainly encouraged by the owners of the Theatre Royal in nearby Crow Street who saw it as an opportunity to increase their falling custom.

The iron works at Coalbrookdale in Shropshire, Britain's first centre of iron casting, was commissioned to cast the bridge following the designs of John Windsor. Construction cost was £3,894. 7s. 11 1/2 d. Wellington Bridge was opened in 1816 to the joy and convenience of generations since.

Open sunrise to sunset the halfpenny toll was collected by officials standing on the railed and roofed-over platforms at either end . The Corporation had to wait until 1917 before Walsh's leases ran their course and the toll could be dispensed with.

It is believed to be one of the world's earliest iron bridges in existence.

Now one of Dublin's most popular sights, it is interesting to note a 1913 quote from Dublin Corporation; "Wellington Bridge is an unsightly structure. It is a narrow footbridge, with a steep gradient and a toll of one halfpenny is made for crossing it. The lease will expire in a few years when a suitable new bridge will be built".

66

TEMPLE BAR c 1900

Fishamble Street

Lord Edward Street

Essex Quay

Exchange Street U

Essex Street West

Cogger Alley

10

Exchange Street Upper

Essex Gate

9

Grattan Bridge

Cork Hill

Parliament Street

Crane Lane

Essex Street East

Crampton Court

Sycamore Street

Coghill's Court

6

5

River Liffey

Wellington Quay

Eustace Street

Dame Street

Temple Lane

Crow Street

Cecilia Street

4

Fownes Street

Temple Bar

7

Cope Street

Crown Alley

Merchant's Arch

3

Halfpenny Bridge

Asdill's Row

2

Crampton Quay

8

Anglesea Street

Bedford Row

Foster Place

Fleet Street

1

Parliament Row

Aston Place

Aston Quay

Prices Lane

College Green

11

O'Connell Bridge

Westmoreland Street

KEY

1 Corporation Electricity Works
2 Webb's
3 Telephone Exchange
4 Catholic University School of Medicine
5 Presbyterian School
6 Friends' Meeting House
7 Commercial Buildings
8 Jury's Hotel
9 Sunlight Chambers
10 Morgan's Court
11 Grattan's Statue

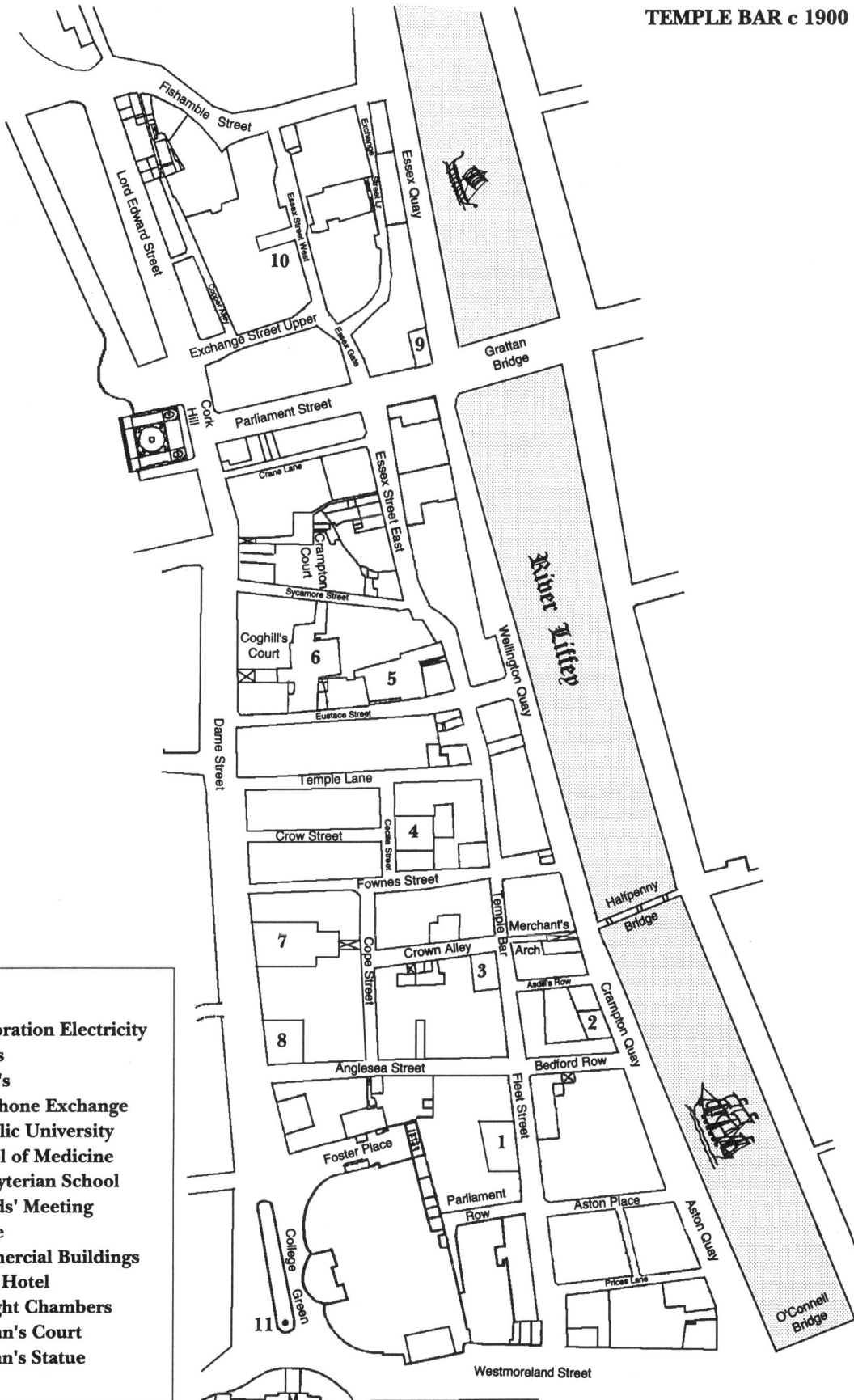

67

THE TWENTIETH CENTURY

When the 20th century dawned nobody would have been able to foresee the changes — political, economic and social — that were to come about in one short generation.

Life continued up to about 1910 much as it had for the previous fifty years. Small and large labour-intensive industries and businesses ensured employment levels were much higher than today. However, with only some notable exceptions, working and living conditions for many were appalling.

Irish nationalism became an issue and events from 1913 to 1923 brought suffering and destruction to the city before political freedom was eventually gained.

Rehousing people living in overcrowded tenements was a priority from the 1920's onwards. The task was enormous but Dublin Corporation undertook a vast programme of building new housing estates. However, there was no replacement for the previous city-centre population (which had been predominantly working class) and the streets became dead at night-time.

To compound the matter, from the 1960's, many traditional craft, distribution and manufacturing businesses abandoned the centre for the industrial estates in the suburbs. All this left areas like Temple Bar very vulnerable to neglect, decay and insensitive re-development, much of which did, in fact, occur.

What happened next is recounted in the introduction to this volume.

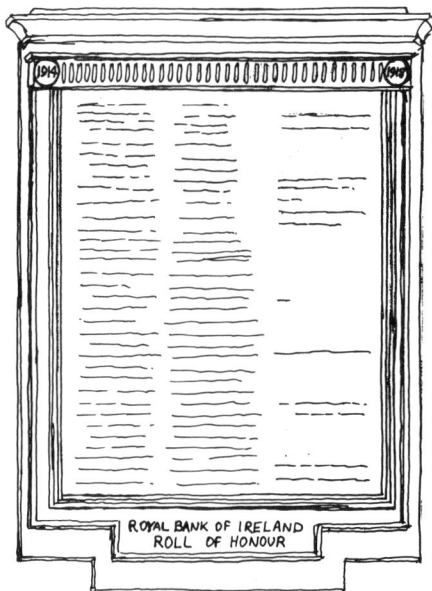

Commemorative Plaque, Allied Irish Bank, Foster Place.
The plaque lists the names of the Royal Bank employees who lost their lives on the battlefields of World War 1.

46/47 Dame Street

9 College Green

The building on the left is sited at the corner of Fownes Street and Dame Street and was built in the last century for the Hibernian Insurance Company. The architects were Deane and Woodworth.

The building on the right was erected in the late nineteenth century for the Patriotic Assurance Company of Ireland.

Both of these buildings were commissioned by Insurance Companies which have long since vacated the premises. They display a Victorian grandeur that insurance firms (thankfully) liked to indulge in, probably to show their customers how safe and reliable they were to deal with.

College Green
Other examples of richly ornamented insurance buildings.

Not all the great edifices of insurance companies survived the building boom of the 1960's and 1970's. These two grand corner buildings at Fownes Street and Foster Place fell for less glorious successors.

Temple Lane Studios

In the 1980's, while still amassing its property portfolio in order to build a huge central city bus station, C.I.E. (the Irish Transport Company) let out several properties at inexpensive, short-term rents. One such property was number 11 Temple Lane, first built as a wholesale tea, wine and spirit store.

   An enthusiastic group of young people took possession of the old warehouse and transformed the almost derelict building into vibrant rehearsal and recording studios.

Royal Bank Porter's Bell
Foster Place.
A relic of the days when this branch of Allied Irish Banks was the Head Office of the Royal Bank (see page 58).

Foundation Stones, Royal Liver Building, Aston Quay.
The Ballast Office was formed in 1707 to earn revenue from providing ballast to ships and to cleanse the port and harbour of silt and obstructions.

Erected c 1800 their headquarters was built at the corner of Westmoreland Street and Aston Quay. Demolished in 1979 a near-replica building was erected on the same spot.

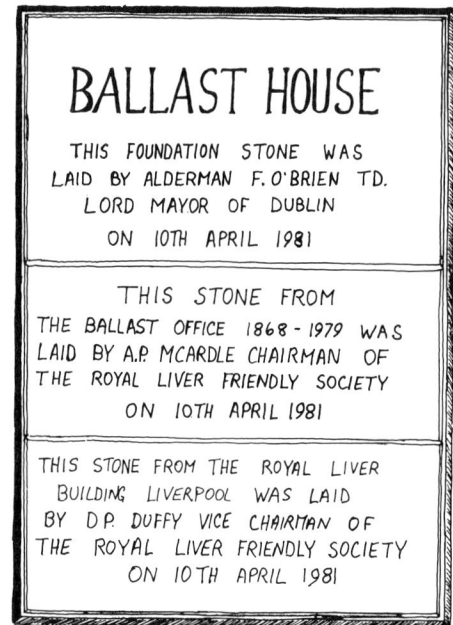

BALLAST HOUSE

THIS FOUNDATION STONE WAS LAID BY ALDERMAN F. O'BRIEN TD. LORD MAYOR OF DUBLIN ON 10TH APRIL 1981

THIS STONE FROM THE BALLAST OFFICE 1868 - 1979 WAS LAID BY A.P. MCARDLE CHAIRMAN OF THE ROYAL LIVER FRIENDLY SOCIETY ON 10TH APRIL 1981

THIS STONE FROM THE ROYAL LIVER BUILDING LIVERPOOL WAS LAID BY D.P. DUFFY VICE CHAIRMAN OF THE ROYAL LIVER FRIENDLY SOCIETY ON 10TH APRIL 1981

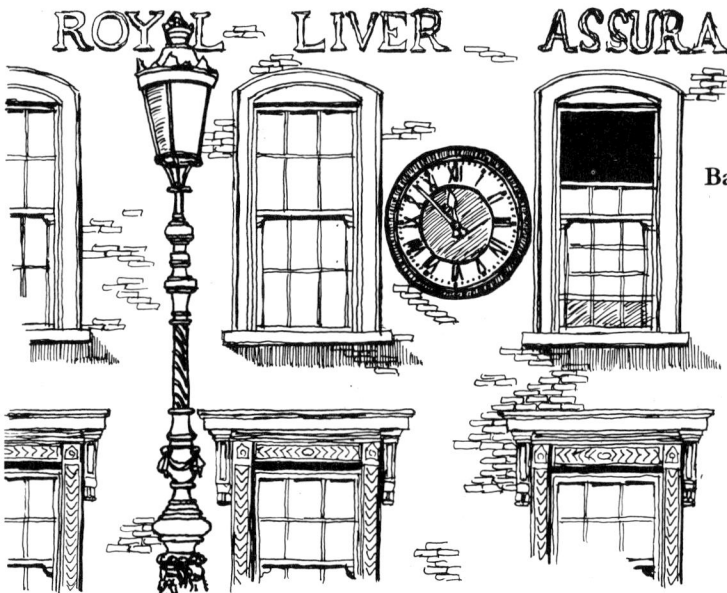

Ballast Office Clock, Royal Liver Buildings, Aston Quay.
A highly accurate clock, connected to Dunsink Observatory, was affixed to the Westmoreland Street facade of the Ballast Office in 1870. This timepiece was in turn linked to a roof apparatus which, by dropping a copper sphere at a predetermined hour, aided mariners in setting ships' chronometers.

The developers of the new Ballast House, the Royal Liver Friendly Society, had the old clock extensively restored and remounted on the Aston Quay side. The timepiece, now linked to a master clock which is synchronised by radio to a Swiss atomic clock, is reputed to be the first of its kind in Ireland. Stored impulses swing the hands to the correct time when current is restored after a power failure and the twice yearly time change is effected automatically.

Chapter 5

STREETS BROAD AND NARROW

PRESENT DAY TEMPLE BAR

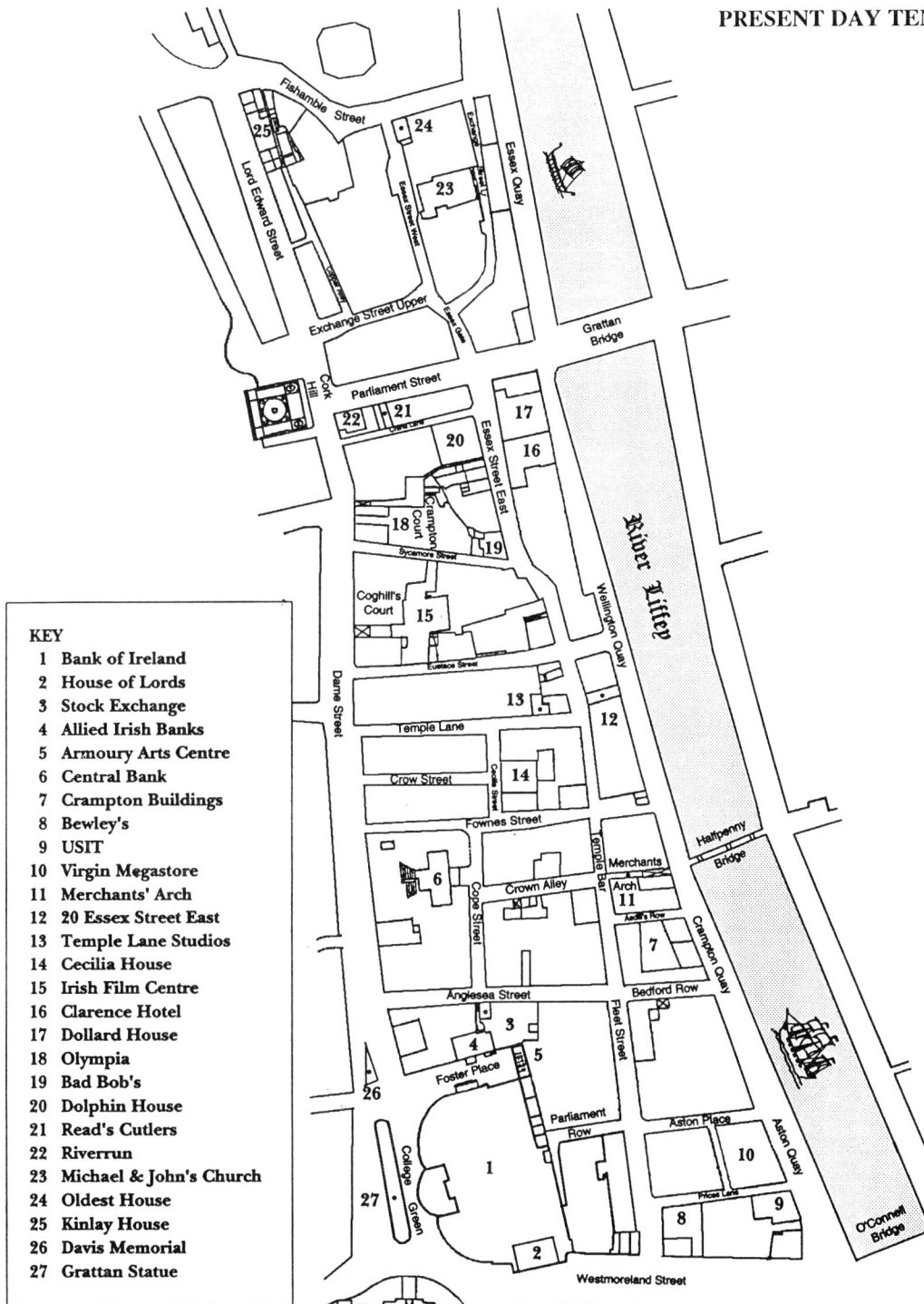

KEY
1 Bank of Ireland
2 House of Lords
3 Stock Exchange
4 Allied Irish Banks
5 Armoury Arts Centre
6 Central Bank
7 Crampton Buildings
8 Bewley's
9 USIT
10 Virgin Megastore
11 Merchants' Arch
12 20 Essex Street East
13 Temple Lane Studios
14 Cecilia House
15 Irish Film Centre
16 Clarence Hotel
17 Dollard House
18 Olympia
19 Bad Bob's
20 Dolphin House
21 Read's Cutlers
22 Riverrun
23 Michael & John's Church
24 Oldest House
25 Kinlay House
26 Davis Memorial
27 Grattan Statue

ADAIR LANE

Origin of name: After Sir Robert Adair who once owned property in the area

Irish name: Lána Uí Dháire.

Date laid down: 1840.

Development: This lane was originally built to accommodate the stables serving the houses on Aston Quay and Fleet Street. Previous to opening up this connection between Aston Place and Price's Lane, ingress to the yards of the houses on this block was through a dead-end alley gained from Price's Lane. Adair Lane still functions solely as a rear entrance to the above named streets.

ASDILL'S ROW

Origin of name: John Asdill, wealthy merchant and agent to the Russian Consul.

Irish name: Rae Asgadail

Date laid down: 1822.

Crampton Buildings, Asdill's Row.

Development: Originally a short row containing houses let out as tenements, the Dublin Artisans' Dwelling Company built a range of 54 flats in 1890. Now called Crampton Buildings, the apartments have recently been tastefully refurbished by the new owners Davis, O'Connor and Company. With their courtyard and iron balconies, the block forms an attractive enclave in an otherwise rather featureless street. The architect was J.W. Beckett.

Crampton Buildings was designed to include small shop units on the street elevations to provide for both the residents themselves and the neighbourhood in general.

ANGLESEA STREET

Origin of name: From Arthur Annesley, 1st Earl of Anglesea.

Irish name: Sráid Mhóna

Date laid down: Originally laid out about 1658 and redeveloped in the 1720's. It first appears in de Gomme-Phillips' Map of 1685 and is marked on Brooking's Map of 1728.

Development: Arthur Annesley acquired a number of leases from the Corporation between the years 1657 and 1662 for "all that part of the strand unto land watermark which abutteth and neareth unto several houses and gardens belonging to Arthur Annesley Esq. situate on the College Green, in the suburbs of the city and adjoining to the seaside there". Much of the early development of this eastern end of Temple Bar and the resultant reclamation from the Liffey foreshore took place during this time.

Anglesea Street was redeveloped in the early part of the 18th century and although it was considered by the standards of the time to be a "wide and commodious thoroughfare" it was usually clogged with rattling coaches, cumbersome carts, throngs of people and sedan chairs weaving in and out as they all plied between the houses of Parliament, Trinity College and the Quays, taverns and residences. All in all probably a nightmare in noise.

Taylors (tailors), dry coopers, hatters, stay-makers, coachmakers and screw pumpmakers were the dominant enterprises of the mid 1700's. One hundred years later the preponderant business in the street was book selling and its ancillary activities.

Arthur Annesley

Arthur Annesley, the first Earl of Anglesea, was born in Fishamble Street in 1614. He was the son of Francis Annesley (1585-1660), Viscount Valentia and Comptroller of the Irish Royal Works. His mother was Anne Perrot, daughter of the Lord Deputy. The Duke of Ormonde surrendered Dublin to him in 1647 and later, as President of the Council of State, he lent his influence to the successful campaign to restore the monarchy for which he was given the title of Earl of Anglesea in 1661.

Some other places named after Arthur Annesley and his descendants are Anglesea Market, Anglesea Row, Annesley Bridge and Annesley Place.

Isaac Sparks (1719 — 1776) a famous comedian of his generation was a resident of Anglesea Street.

The early poetic efforts of Thomas Moore first appeared in the "Anthologia Hibernica", which was published by Mercier & Co. from Number 31 between 1793 and 1794.

Thomas Cooley (1740-1784) architect of the City Hall, the Hibernian Marine School, Newgate Prison and the Records Office of the Four Courts, lived in Anglesea Street and died of bilious fever in his home.

Number 6 was the residence of Thomas Perry (died 1818) a master violin maker often described as the Irish Stradivarius. In partnership with his son-in-law William Wilkinson, he subsequently moved shop to Number 4 (which was later to become part of Jury's Hotel), and the business continued here until 1839. Perry's violins are now much sought after all over the world.

The Dublin Stock Exchange No.28 .

The frontage is composed of white fire brick with dressings of grey granite (see also page 97).

Bloom's Hotel, Anglesea Street.

Bloom's Hotel was once part of the famed Jury's Hotel Group. While Jury's fronted onto College Green the only expansion possible to the hotel was down Anglesea Street. Property from College Green down to Cope Street was acquired from the 1840's down to 1962 when the extension now known as Bloom's Hotel was opened on the site of William Hogg's wholesale warehouse. Jury's moved to Ballsbridge in 1973 and the extension became an hotel in its own right and was named after Leopold Bloom, a character in James Joyce's "Ulysses".

Number 7 is the National Office of the Scouting Association of Ireland, founded in 1908, which currently has 16,000 members. Dublin claims the oldest troop of sea scouts in the world based at Dollymount.

ASTON PLACE

Origin of name: See Aston Quay, page 78.

Irish name: Plás Astuin.

Former name: Lee's Lane.

Date laid down: 1728, renamed in 1885.

Development: Once a busy narrow laneway containing a variety of small businesses and houses, it provided a useful secondary connection to Aston Quay from Fleet Street. By the mid 1850's the residences were mostly let out as tenements. John Ward, a famous violin maker of the mid 1700's, lived here. He died in 1769.

In the early part of this century the street was considered to be a book browsers' paradise with its coterie of second-hand booksellers. Nothing of this tradition now remains. The well known Three Candles Print premises was sold in 1991 for use as a headquarters and other facilities to the Union of Students in Ireland (USI).

The "Sign of the Times" are extracts from "The Freeman's Journal" which was printed in Crane Lane in the 1780's. The paper was in existence from 1763-1924. These extracts demonstrate life in Dublin in the eighteenth century and would have been typical of life in Temple Bar at the time.

Sign of the Times

**By the KING'S PATENT
CAKES for making of SHINING
LIQUID BLACKING**

For SHOES, BOOTS etc.

Agent James Bourfiquot, Essex Bridge, Dublin.

These Cakes make, by the Addition of Water only, a most excellent Shining Liquid Blacking, much superior to any hitherto known: It gives the finest Black, and most beautiful Gloss to the Leather, yet never renders it stiff or hard, but, on the contrary, prevents it cracking, and preserves it soft and pliable to the very last, whereby it is rendered more agreeable to the Wearer, as well as much more durable, and the Shoes that are blacked with it, will neither soil the Fingers in putting on, not the Stockings in Wearing.

The patentee intreats all Persons, who are curious in Blacking, to take the Trouble of seeing that the Cakes bought for their Use have a Label pasted on them, with the following Inscription: BY THE KING'S PATENT, CAKES for Shining Liquid Blacking, prepared by WILLIAM BAYLEY. He having discovered that their great Reputation has occasioned many Persons to counterfeit them, some of whom have been prosecuted; but as there are still others whose Names he cannot find out, who continue the fraud, and impose upon the Public, he hopes this caution will be attended to.

The Freeman's Journal 9 — 11 June 1778.

ASTON QUAY

Origin of name: Usually thought to be named after Henry Aston, merchant and one time Lord Mayor, to whom this area of city land was let in 1672. He enclosed the site from the river and built a Quay.

Irish name: Cé Astuin.

Date laid down: Early 1700's. It was named as Aston Quay from 1708.

Development: In 1756 it still included the present Burgh Quay up to Hawkins Street. Henry Aston's son, also Henry, rebuilt most of the houses on the Quay and on Fleet Street in 1760. This was in the parish of St. Mark's which was created in 1708 from the old St. Andrew's parish and was one of the poorest areas in the city. According to Whitelaw's census of 1798, the highest house occupancy rate was on the quays.

Merchants and grocers were the predominant traders in the 18th century. In 1850 among the businesses listed were fringe and tassel makers, florists, glass menders, ironmongers, vintners, watchmakers, shoemakers and a dealer in sweetmeats. At number 7 the same family carried out a varied portfolio which included the functions of assay master, dentistry and proprietor of a ladies day school.

From Shaw's City Pictorial Directory 1850.

USIT (Union of Students in Ireland Travel Company), Aston Quay.

Formerly the premises of Hodges Hardware and whose garage was once the Coach House on the Dublin — Cork route, this building was bought in 1946 to become the headquarters of Irish Shipping. It passed to the Irish Continental Line in 1974 and subsequently to USIT in 1987. USIT is the second largest youth and travel organisation in the world.

Virgin Megastore, Aston Quay.

This building started life in the first half of the 19th century as McBirney, Collis & Co. Silk Merchants & Drapers and later became a notable department store. By the 1970's its location had isolated it from the mainstream shopping streets and for that and other reasons its fortunes declined and the firm closed its doors in the 1980's. It was subsequently bought by the Virgin Group.

Sign of the Times

About Four o'Clock in the Morning Mr Dennis Callen, of Ormond-market, Butcher, was so dangerously wounded by a party of Ruffians in Smock-Alley, that he died soon after; several Persons were apprehended and lodged in Newgate.

The Freeman's Journal 10 — 14 January 1768.

BEDFORD LANE

Origin of name: From John Russell, the 4th Duke of Bedford, Lord Lieutenant 1757-1761.

Irish name: Lána Bedford.

Date laid down: 1760's.

Development: Designed solely for access to stables and sheds. Today there is little to interest the passerby.

BEDFORD ROW

Origin of name: See Bedford Lane.

Irish name: Rae Bedford.

Former name: Porter's Row.

Date laid down: 1760's.

Development: Its history is undistinguished. Wilson's Directory of 1762 notes only one business, that of Grace, the butcher. Shaw's directory of 1850 lists a fancy painter, a fringe and tassel manufacturer, a tin plate worker, some bootmakers and provision dealers. The rest of the property was let in tenements. The most significant building today is the large switching station of the Electricity Supply Board.

Clohissy's Bookshop that once stood at No. 10 and No. 11 is where Stephen Dedalus, in James Joyce's "Ulysses", rummaged through the bookcarts looking for one of his pawned school prizes.

CECILIA STREET

Origin of name: Named after Cecilia Fownes, a member of the famous family who developed much of this area.

Irish name: Sráid Shisile.

Former name: Was part of Crow Street until renamed in 1766.

Date laid down: Early 17th century.

Development: Present day Cecilia House stands on what was once the site of the medieval friary of the Order of Augustinian Hermits (see Crow Street). Before the land was developed in the 17th century the ground behind Cecilia Street would have marked the southern shore line of the Liffey.

Cecilia Street is most famous for two of its former institutions; the Crow Street Theatre and the Catholic University School of Medicine both of which occupied what is now Cecilia House. The "Dublin Penny Journal", a weekly newspaper, was published from Cecilia Street in the mid 1830's.

Cecilia House

The former School of Medicine building is now owned by John J. Cooke & Son, a jewellery and silverware manufacturing company. Cooke's started over 40 years ago in neighbouring Fownes Street on a site now occupied by the Central Bank.

Poney Races, at the Theatre Royal, Crow-Street.

Crow Street Theatre

In 1730 the newly founded Dublin Academy of Music built the Crow Street Music Hall "for the practice of Italian music". The opening show was "Ridotto". A year later a riot in the Hall resulted in the army killing several of the mob. Spranger Barry (a former head of the Covent Garden Theatre in London) leased the Music Hall in 1757, had it demolished and built the new 2,000 seat Crow Street Theatre at a cost of £22,000, to rival that of Drury Lane. Renamed the Theatre Royal it gained a European-wide reputation and many noted performers acted here. Various owners followed over the years, some also owning rival theatres such as Smock Alley and the Playhouse in Capel Street.

On several successive occasions the time-honoured custom of rioting in Dublin theatres resulted in several deaths and the near destruction of the Crow Street premises but again and again it made a come-back.

In 1798 Frederick E. "Buck" Jones, having purchased and improved it, re-opened the Theatre Royal with a performance of "The Merchant of Venice". Because of a curfew imposed as a result of the 1798 rebellion he suffered financial ruin. (Jones's Road beside Croke Park, was built by him to gain entrance to his grand residence, Clonliffe House, which he had already lost when he died penniless in 1834).

The theatre, rocked by more riots, especially in 1819, finally closed in 1820 to the echoes of "Richard III". A portion of the site was purchased in 1836 by the Company of the Apothecaries Hall for their medical school. They were succeeded by the Catholic University School of Medicine in 1855.

COLLEGE GREEN

Origin of name: Named after Trinity College, founded during the reign of Queen Elizabeth in 1592.

Irish name: Faiche an Choláiste.

Former name: Hoggen Green (named after the convent of St. Mary de Hogge established 1156 at present day Trinity Street).

Date laid down: College Green gradually evolved from the Middle Ages but was established in a cohesive manner from 1592 .

Development: It is known that the history of College Green goes back even further than medieval days because megalithic burial grounds were levelled during construction in the 1650's. The first building of any significance was the Augustinian Monastery of All Hallows which was founded in 1166 on the land where Trinity College is now situated. Hoggen Green was an area of common pastureland which stretched from All Hallows halfway up Dame Street. The river Steine flowed through it at the eastern end.

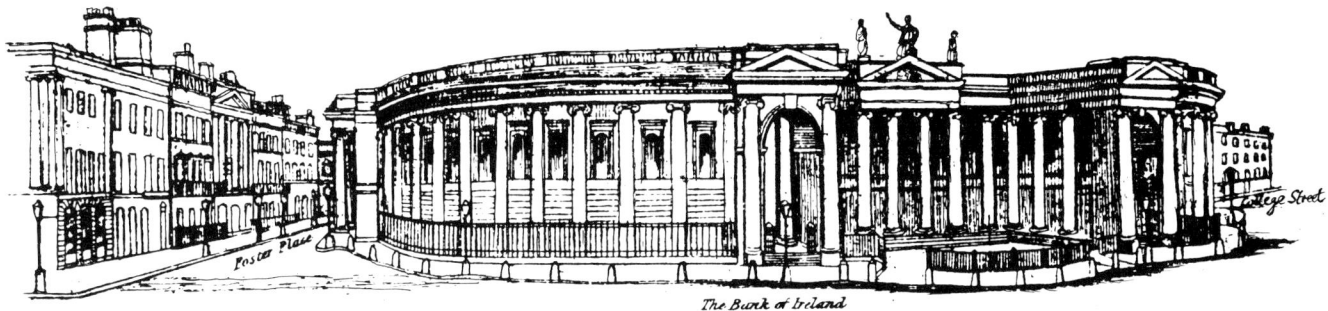

The Bank of Ireland

Henry Shaw's New City Pictorial Directory 1850

The opening of Trinity College encouraged the arrival of some other institutions to the area. One of the first was a bridewell or prison which was built in front of Trinity, no doubt to remind the boisterous students to keep some control on their exuberances. Another was Sir Thomas Carey's Hospital. It was never used as such, but was converted into courtrooms (1605), later becoming Chichester House. Sir John Borace, the Lord Justice, was the next occupant and during his tenancy the Privy Council sat here. In 1685 Chichester House was purchased by the Crown for use as a Parliament building and so commenced a new era for College Green and indeed for the whole of Dublin.

Daly's Club, a gambling mecca for gentlemen and nobility was conveniently opened next door to the Parliament in 1789.

On the rest of College Green, contemporaneous with the House of Parliament, were found some trades which were most likely patronised by the Lords and elected personages; a tobacconist, grocer, cardmaker, saddler, jeweller and gunsmith. As wide a variety of businesses as can be imagined moved in by the 1850's and within a few more decades College Green settled down as a banking and insurance centre.

Sadly missed by an older generation is Jury's Hotel which stood at the West corner of College Green and Anglesea Street. Starting as a commercial lodgings at number 7 in 1839 it went on to become one of the city's premier hotels. In 1973 Jury's transferred to Ballsbridge and remarkably, the hotel's Victorian long bar was sold as one lot and bought by the U.B.S. Bank of Switzerland and re-erected in their premises at Pelikan Strasse, Zurich.

Sign of the Times

GOTTLEIB SIMON KIRCHNER

FURRIER, from Prussia

Removed from No. 17 to No. 11 College-green, Dublin in order to carry on his business most extensively

Returns his most sincere thanks to the Nobility, Gentry and Public in general, for their kind encouragement since his commencement in business. He has just imported from Russia and Siberia a large assortment of Linings and Trimmings of real Siberia Ermine, different colours, blue, green, white.

He has a large quantity of the best Eider Down.

He flatters himself that none in the kingdom can undersell him, as he has the best connections abroad. The goods that are bought from him may be depended upon to being well manufactured.

N.B. An Apprentice wanted.

A First Floor to be let, unfurnished.

The Freeman's Journal 19 — 21 December 1780.

Grattan Statue.

Unveiled in 1876, the sculptor was John Henry Foley whose work includes Burke and Goldsmith in front of Trinity College and Sir Benjamin Guinness outside St. Patrick's Cathedral. His work also included the famous equestrian statue of General Viscount Hugh Gough (blown up 23rd July 1957) in the Phoenix Park. His most famous work, however, is not in Dublin but in London — the gigantic bronze gilt statue of the Prince Consort, centre piece of the Albert Memorial opposite the Royal Albert Hall, unveiled in 1876. The Albert statue in the Leinster House lawn is also his. Foley was born in Dublin in 1818 near Amiens Street. He attended the RDS Art School.

Henry Grattan was born in Dublin in 1746 and entered the Irish Parliament when he was 29. He proved to be a fiery orator and became leader of the opposition Liberal Party. He wanted Ireland to have a measure of legislative freedom and an end put to trade restrictions. He did not, however, envisage a break with the British Crown as such.

With his powerful rhetoric, in what became popularly known as Grattan's Parliament, his dreams began to take shape only to be cruelly dashed by the Act of Union in 1800. After the dissolution of Parliament he received a generous financial settlement from the authorities and on his death, in what some might consider a purely political exercise, he was accorded the honour of burial in Westminster Abbey.

Davis Memorial.

The memorial honours patriot and poet Thomas Davis (1814 — 1845). The sculptor of the bronze figures of Davis and his trumpeting heralds was Edward Delaney. The granite tablets illustrate with bronze reliefs the poetry of Davis and a depiction of the Irish Famine. The statue stands near the site where once the equestrian statue of King William III was placed. The latter was erected in 1701 and it was frequently abused and mutilated before being finally blown up in 1929.

Sign of the Times

At Night a numerous Mob associated for the Purpose of ravaging Houses of ill Fame, in this city and Suburbs. They divided themselves into different Parties, and perambulated the Town all Night and the succeeding Day, in which short Period they sacked about 40 Houses. The Devastation committed upon this occasion not withstanding the remarkable industry of our Magistrates, consisting of twenty eight, to prevent It, and who exerted themselves with their usual spirit and Alacrity, cannot be equalled by any one similar Circumstance in the Memory of Man, before or since the memorable Military Insurrection on the 6th and 7th of August, 1765, when Newgate was broke open, and upwards of seventy Fellows, &c. were let loose upon the Public; However after the Damages to the Landlords and Tenants, were sustained to the Amount of at least 20,000L . Forty of the Rioters were apprehended by the Lord Mayor and Sheriffs (most of whom were found fatigued after their Day's Hard Labour, intoxicated with Liquor) at Ringsend, where they finished their Work, by destroying two other Houses, as they were conducted to Newgate, where they now remain — miserable Objects indeed. Who would not wish to live in the free City! Sensible and spirited Magistrates!

The Freeman's Journal 10 — 14 June 1768.

At Night Mr. Mulcahy, of Fishamble Street, Publican, remarkable for his Performances on the Bag pipes, fell into the Liffey at Ormond Quay, and was unfortunately drowned.

The Freeman's Journal 8 April 1769.

At a meeting of the Church Wardens and Directors of the Watch of the several Parishes within the Liberties of the City of Dublin, at the Tholsel, on Friday the 10th April, 1772, pursuant to Advertisement.

The Right Hon. the Lord Mayor in the Chair,
the following Resolutions were unanimously agreed to.

Resolved, That it be recommended to the several Parishes, to offer a Reward for apprehending and prosecuting Street Robbers.

Resolved, That it would tend to preserve public Peace, if the Directors of the Watch of the respective Parishes would patrol the several Streets, and of their Districts, and apprehend disorderly Persons.

Resolved, That increasing the Number of able Watchmen in each Parish, as far as such Parish could afford, would tend to prevent Robberies and Disturbance in the City.

The Freeman's Journal 14 — 16 April 1772.

The House of Parliament

The first Irish Parliament after the Restoration of Charles II met in Chichester House in May 1661. This venue was not ideal and by the 1720's the advanced decay of the house convinced the members to demolish it and order a new structure of some magnificence to replace it.

Edward Lovett Pearce was appointed architect and the foundation stone was laid in 1728. In attendance were Pearce, the Lords Justice, nobility, Members of Parliament, Yeomen of the Guard and detachments of dragoons and foot. A purse with 21 guineas was placed on top of the stone which "the architect distributed among the craftsmen to drink towards the health of their Majesties". A decade passed before work was completed.

The new building was the world's first to be designed specifically as a two chamber legislature. The octagonal shaped House of Commons was crowned by a lofty dome and the proceedings could be watched by up to 700 spectators in the upper galleries.

The Lords and Members also had their priorities right and provided themselves with ample kitchens equipped "with a large apparatus for good eating". In the dining rooms "all distinctions as to Government or opposing parties were totally laid aside; harmony, wit, wine and good humour reigning triumphant".

A further effort to increase their creature comforts backfired when a newly installed but defective heating system caused a fire which destroyed the Commons Chamber in 1792. By the time it was rebuilt the Parliament had less than four years to run before it was dissolved by the Act of Union in 1800.

Three of Dublin's greatest architects were involved in expanding or readapting the building; James Gandon (East portico 1785), Robert Parke (Foster Place portico 1797) and Francis Johnston (curving screen wall and armoury in Foster Place and major interior alterations 1803). Edward Smyth carved the statues of Fidelity, Hibernia and Commerce.

Former Houses of Parliament, now Bank of Ireland, College Green.

COPE STREET

Origin of name: From Robert Cope (died 1748) who married Elizabeth, the daughter of Sir William Fownes. He also had Cope Street North (now Talbot Street) named after him.

Irish name: Sráid Cope.

Date laid down: Evolved during the 17th century development of the district and was named Cope Street circa 1756, when some new building had commenced.

Development; An unremarkable street in many ways it has little claim to fame or notoriety. Warehouses and merchants were its stock trade. Half of the southern side of the street was demolished in the 1970's to make way for the Central Bank.

Sign of the Times

> A publican on Temple-bar, having sent a Boy for some Glauber Salts, by Mistake had a Quantity of Arsenic sent him, which he took; but the Effects soon appearing, he drank some Sallad Oil, which made him evacuate the Dose, and preserved his Life.
>
> *The Freeman's Journal* 28 — 31 March 1767.

COPPER ALLEY

Origin of name: It received its name from Lady Alice Fenton, widow of Sir Geoffrey Fenton, Secretary of State 1581 — 1608. She was famous for distributing copper money to the poor from her house which was located nearby.

Irish name: Scabhat an Chopair.

Former name: Preston's Lane (15th Century) from the Preston family who had property on the north side of Copper Alley.

Date laid down: 16th century.

Development: Copper Alley developed gradually from the gardens and orchards just inside the city wall. Starting as a mere lane it had by the 17th century become an important and thriving street. It ran from Fishamble Street to Blind Quay (Upper Exchange Street) and was served by connections from Castle Street and Smock Alley (West Essex Street).

The main exit from the Fishamble Street Music Hall led into Copper Alley which allowed for a very civilised and ordered evacuation. Carriages first deposited their passengers outside the hall and then proceeded around the corner and lined up to await the final curtain.

The street had its share of taverns including the Red Lion Tavern, a haunt of one-time conspirators and bored carriage drivers! A number of distinguished 18th century printing houses traded from Copper Alley including Andrew Cook, the King's Printer General for Ireland (1673 — 1727).

The family of Catherine McAuley, foundress of the Sisters of Mercy, lived in Copper Alley before moving to Fishamble Street in the late 1700's.

In 1762 no less than 8 shoemakers are listed as having lived there, not altogether surprising given the state of road surfaces at that time. The significance of the street was diminishing by the 1850's when bone yards, back street tailors and storage yards appeared. The final death knell came with the opening of the new Lord Edward Street in 1886. To add insult to mortal injury the opening onto Fishamble Street was recently finally blocked off.

Copper Alley.
From a painting by Alexander Williams, R.H.A.

CORK HILL

Origin of name: From Richard Boyle, 1st. Earl of Cork.

Irish name: Cnoc Corcaigh.

Date laid down: Mid 1600's.

Development: One of the first mansions to be built outside the confines of the city walls was that built by Richard Boyle around 1600. He chose the site of the demolished medieval church of St. Mary del Dam.

Other houses soon followed and over the next hundred years the street grew in importance due to its close proximity to Dublin Castle. Two of the 19th century shops here were bonnet warehouses, no doubt aimed at the high fashion ladies who frequented the soirees in Dublin Castle. Originally T-shaped, it was to suffer major dissection on two occasions. The first was the opening of Parliament Street when in the 1760's many of the houses were levelled to open up space for the new avenue and the building of the Royal Exchange. The second major alteration occurred with the opening of Lord Edward Street.

In 1735 the notable Hell Fire Club was founded in the Cork Hill Eagle Tavern. Another fashionable meeting place in the 18th century was Lucas' Coffee House. It was related at the time that "pedestrians passing Cork Hill after dark were frequently insulted and maltreated by the numerous chairmen surrounding the entrances to both of these establishments".

Henry Shaw's New City Pictorial Directory 1850

CRAMPTON COURT

Origin of name: From Philip Crampton (see Crampton Quay).

Irish name: Cúirt Crampton.

Former name: Horse Guard Yard.

Date laid down: 1745.

Development: Before the unit was removed to Dublin Castle in the early 18th century, the Horse Guard Barracks was situated on this site. The ground was then sold to Philip Crampton who developed Crampton Court.

Crampton had his residence here and he and the other residents were joined by a variety of merchants and several members of the rapidly growing insurance community. The latter moved to the Commercial Buildings when they were opened in 1799 and in their place there arrived watchmakers, booksellers, jewellers and other assorted trades.

Fifty years later the premises of a shell fish dealer, a tailor, a preparer of soda water, a gin maker, a vintner and 5 tenements formed the panorama. Around this time the firm of Rathborne Candles, reputedly the world's oldest chandlers (over 500 years old and still going strong at East Wall Road), was located here.

In this century, Crampton Court became sadly derelict and by the 1970's all the houses had been demolished. Crampton Court, once the main entrance to the Olympia Theatre, has been relegated to the side entrance. The winding laneway still connects Dame Street with Essex Street East.

Sign of the Times

The many fatal Calamities which happen by Fire in this Metropolis, evidently shows the Necessity there is for the Public to be guarded against such Danger, by having their Property insured, which may be done at a small Expence, in the Office of the Hibernian Insurance Company against Fire, in Crampton-court, where due Attendance is given.

The Freeman's Journal 23 — 25 June 1778.

The famous Mrs BERNARD, Dentist, from Berlin,

Most respectfully acquaints the Public, that she has appointed Mr. Butler, Grocer, No. 57 Dame Street, the only Vendor in Ireland for her excellent Liquid for curing all Disorders incident to the Teeth and Gums, remarkable for curing the Scurvy in the Gums, and in a short Time removes the most offensive Breath. Also, by virtue of said Liquid, the Gums adhere to the Teeth, it renders them as white as Alebaster, and preserves the Enamel, not withstanding their being much impaired.

The Freeman's Journal 12 — 14 November 1776.

CRAMPTON QUAY

Origin of name: From Philip Crampton (1696-1792).

Irish name: Cé Crampton.

Date laid down: 1766

Development: Until the opening of Wellington Quay in 1816 there was no riverfront connection between Crampton Quay and the Custom House Quay further upriver. Crampton Quay has the distinction of being the shortest quay along the Liffey.

As a dockside, prior to the opening of Carlisle (O'Connell) Bridge in 1798, Crampton Quay was a landing stage for salt and potato cargoes.

In the 19th century a number of foreign consulates opened offices along the quays and in the adjoining streets. Number 3 housed the Spanish Consul around 1850.

Sir Philip Crampton

Philip Crampton was a wealthy bookseller who also dabbled in property acquisition. He acquired what was later to become Crampton Court, off Dame Street. Crampton filled the position of City Sheriff for a period, during which, in 1755, he was honoured for helping to suppress gambling houses in the city. In 1758 he was elected Lord Mayor. He died at the ripe old age of ninety six, quite an achievement when the average life expectancy was only in the sixties.

CRANE LANE

Origin of name: Named after the public crane which was placed on the old Custom House Quay at the end of this street.

Irish name: Lána an Chraein.

Date laid down: Circa 1620. The western side was built in 1762.

Development: The name of the street is the sole reminder of the 18th century docks and Custom House located at the Custom House Quay (now the western end of Wellington Quay). This narrow thoroughfare was once a primary route to Dublin Castle before Parliament Street was built.

The street had the usual mix of 18th century trading establishments including a couple of cutlers, and not-so-posh residences many of which converted into tenements in the last century. As might be expected on a street serving dockland, there were a number of taverns situated here including the "Bear Tavern". From 1782 the "Freeman's Journal" was printed at the works of Forbes Ross, Crane Lane.

The city's first Jewish synagogue was opened in Crane Lane around 1663.

Sign of the Times

STOPPED

By Mr. Justice Drury, supposed to have been stolen, the Under-perch of a Carriage, with the Iron-work; two new Curricle Springs; a large Log of Fustick, used by Dyers, and two Bridles and Saddles.

Whoever can prove the above Articles to be their Property, may have them, by applying to the above Magistrate, at No. 116, Lower Coombe.

The Freeman's Journal 16 — 19 September 1799.

It is with the highest Pleasure we can assure the Public, that the Harvest is better, and in greater Plenty, than hath been known for many Years past; the Corn in general is fuller, the Hay better, and the Potatoes far exceeding in Size and Goodness any that have been known in this Kingdom.

The Freeman's Journal 5 — 8 September 1767.

CROWN ALLEY

Origin of name: Possibly originates from a tavern displaying the sign of The Crown.

Irish name: Scabhat na Crónach.

Date laid down: 1728.

Development: The street originally extended all the way to Dame Street until a portion (from Cope Street) was taken away to allow for the erection of the Commercial Buildings in 1796. The name "Alley" in Medieval and Georgian parlance usually described a narrow passage leading down to a river. Other examples are: Faddle Alley (Poddle River), Thundercut Alley (Bradogue River), Ball Alley (Dodder River) etc.

Even though the street is relatively insignificant historically, it derives its modern importance as a pedestrian link between the North and South city business and shopping districts.

On what is probably one of the most vibrant and best known streets of Temple Bar, former shops and merchant wholesale warehouses have been transformed into restaurants, eateries, boutiques and a music venue in Oman's splendidly restored erstwhile furniture removal warehouse (see pages 65 and 99).

The Sign of the Crown

Sign of the Times

A Boy was detected picking Pockets at the Gallery Door of the Theatre Royal, Crow Street, and underwent the severe Discipline of Ducking.

The Same Night a Gentleman was attacked by Three Footpads opposite Mercer's Hospital, but making a stout Resistance, the Fellows made off without their Booty.

The Freeman's Journal 26 — 29 December 1767.

The State Lottery office was situated on the outskirts of Temple Bar.

In all the different Schemes, now selling at Gilbert and Cos. STATE LOTTERY OFFICE, No. 26 Great George's Street, where Adventurers will receive the earliest intelligence of their Success. Tickets bought at said office registered gratis, and ready Money for Prizes.

CROW STREET

Origin of name: From William Crow, owner of the site of the suppressed Monastery of St. Augustine. He was appointed in 1597 to the glorious title of Chirographer & Chief Prothonotary to the Court of Common Pleas.

Irish name: Sráid Chró.

Date laid down: 1627, rebuilt in 1756.

Development: Crow built his house here and ran a convenient lane down to the Liffey.

The Dublin Resource Centre. No. 6 is a fine example of a Victorian shopfront. The premises was originally a bookmaker and printer.

St. Augustine's Monastery (1259 — 1537) stood on the site of what is now Cecilia Street and a portion of present Crow Street. The monastery was probably built up to the river and most likely had its own landing stage. It was suppressed in 1537. The site was granted by Henry VIII to Walter Tyrrel and from whose descendants William Crow acquired the land. The demolition of St. Augustine's prompted the easterly development of the 16th century town. The Government in the mid 1600's took over Crow's house and turned it into offices aptly renaming it the Crow's Nest. The offices included the Survey of the Fortified Irish Lands. The Dublin Philosophical Society (predecessor to the Royal Dublin Society) once had its headquarters here and established a laboratory, museum and botanic gardens in 1684.

The Crow Street Theatre (see Cecilia Street) was erected on the section of Crow Street which was renamed Cecilia Street in 1766.

Staymakers, perukemakers, a house painter and an upholder plied their trades here in the 18th century. They were replaced in the 19th century by mostly tailors and engravers.

A resident of the street was Hugh Douglas Hamilton. Born in 1739, son of a wig-maker, Hamilton went on to become an eminent portrait painter and many of his works are in the National Gallery.

The Holy Faith Sisters operated a school at No. 10 from 1861 until 1873 when they moved to Clarendon Street (the site of the present Westbury Hotel).

Alex Thom & Co., printers of the famous Thom's Directories since 1844 (which are still being printed today), took offices at No. 2 Crow Street after their Abbey Street offices were destroyed in the 1916 Rising and they remained there until the 1960's.

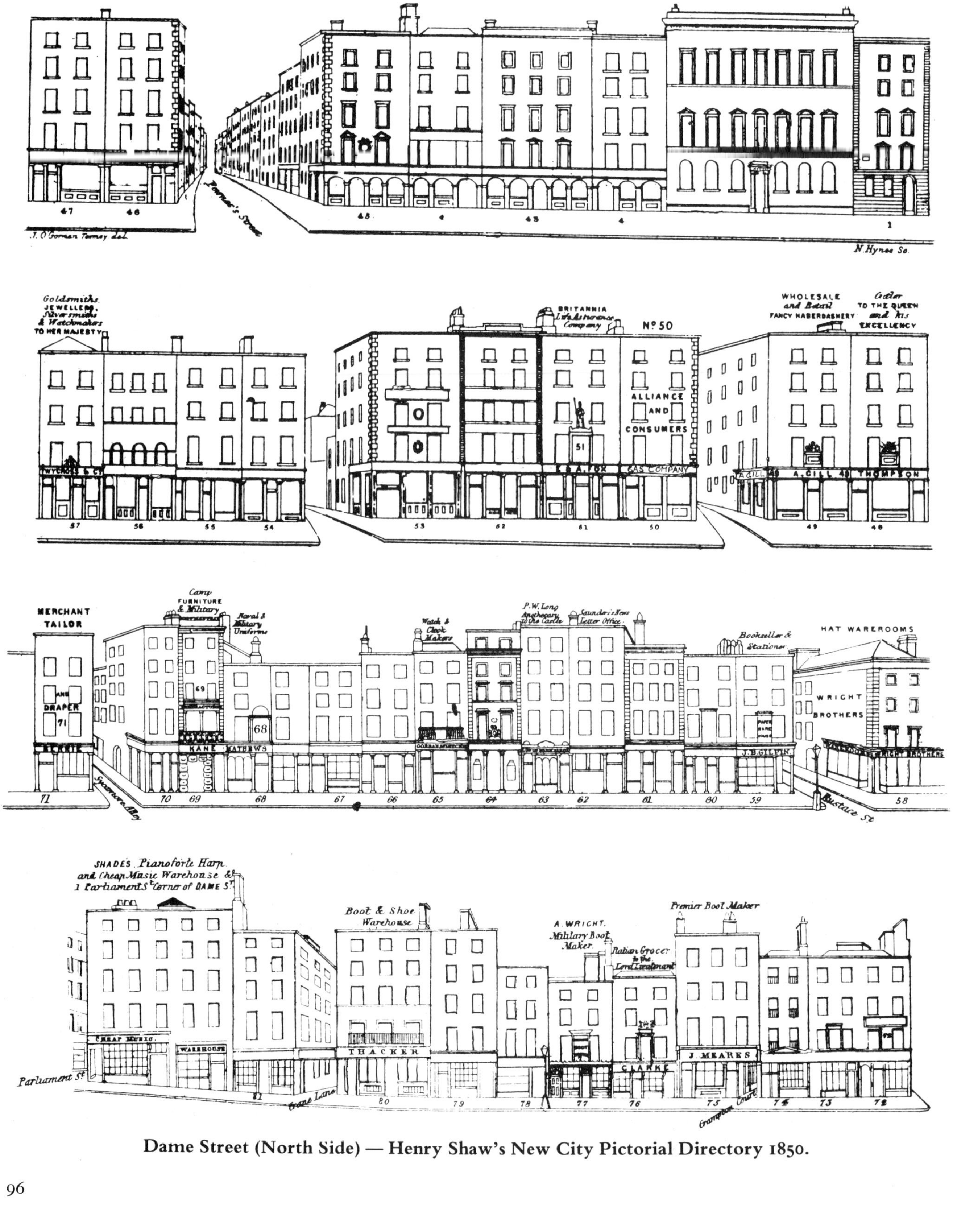

47 46 43 4 45 4 1

J. O'Gorman Foray del. N Hynes Sc.

Goldsmiths, JEWELLERS Silversmiths & Watchmakers TO HER MAJESTY

BRITANNIA Life Assurance Company Nº 50

ALLIANCE AND CONSUMERS

WHOLESALE and Retail FANCY HABERDASHERY

Cutler TO THE QUEEN and His EXCELLENCY

TWYCROSS & Cº

S.A.FOX GAS COMPANY

A.GILL 49 A.GILL 49 THOMPSON

57 56 55 54 53 52 51 50 49 48

MERCHANT TAILOR

Camp FURNITURE & Military Warehouse

Naval & Military Uniforms

Watch & Clock Makers

P.W. Long Apothecary to the Castle

Saunders's News Letter Office

Bookseller & Stationer

HAT WAREROOMS

AND DRAPER 71

69

68

KANE MATHEWS

GORMAN & COOPER

NEW MEDICAL

WRIGHT BROTHERS

J.B.GILPIN

71 70 69 68 67 66 65 64 63 62 61 60 59 58

SHADES, Pianoforte Harp and Cheap Music Warehouse & 1 Parliament Sᵗ Corner of DAME Sᵗ

Boot & Shoe Warehouse

A. WRIGHT. Military Boot Maker

Italian Grocer to the Lord Lieutenant

Premier Boot Maker

CHEAP MUSIC WAREHOUSE

THACKER

CLARKE

J. MEARS

Parliament Sᵗ

71 80 79 78 77 76 75 74 73 72

Dame Street (North Side) — Henry Shaw's New City Pictorial Directory 1850.

96

Stock Exchange, Anglesea Street.

This pen and wash drawing depicts the market floor of the Dublin Stock Exchange, Anglesea Street where today trading takes place twice daily at 9.30 am and again at 2.15 pm.

Originally founded in 1799, the Dublin Stock Exchange first met in the Royal Exchange's (now the City Hall) Coffee House before moving to the Commercial Buildings in Dame Street. It moved to its present building in 1878. The impressive floor of the Exchange, with its Victorian ambience, albeit equipped with computer moniters, saw its centralised role somewhat diminished after the "Big Bang" in October 1986 when trading activity accelerated to highly complex computerised brokers dealing rooms scattered around the city. The interior is destined to survive as it has been placed on Dublin Corporation's Preservation List.

Architects were Messrs. Miller & Symes of Great Brunswick (Pearse) Street. Contractor was George Meyers of Richmond Street.

The Bank of Ireland, College Green.

The Bank of Ireland bought the Old Parliament House in 1802 and had it converted for its own use. While it is regrettable that the House of Commons interior was demolished (as required by the sale agreement) the replacement is equally outstanding. However, the House of Lords (page 87) has remained intact and its preservation, along with the original mace and wall tapestries, makes it unique as it is possibly Europe's oldest legislature accommodation still in its original condition.

The Bank of Ireland was founded in Mary's Abbey (near the Four Courts) in 1783. It negotiated a move to the defunct Parliament House in 1803 and reopened here in 1808. It remained the bank's Head Office until the mid 1960's and it is still the principal Dublin branch. Until the 1940's the Bank of Ireland minted and printed Ireland's currency.

In the early 1800's John Oldham, a Dublin engraver, invented a new method of printing bank notes. At that time, the forgery of bank notes was widespread and Oldham developed a system of numbering which impressed the Bank of Ireland and he was appointed engineer and chief engraver. The method was so successful that the Bank of England made him their printer. He later went on to develop a paddle wheel for steam powered ships. He died in 1840.

In 1971 the Bank of Ireland set new standards for careful restoration when it commenced cleaning and replacing the dirt-encrusted and damaged exterior stonework. Over the south pediment, the head of Edward Smyth's statues of Commerce, Fidelity and Hibernia were newly carved by Paddy Roe of Sandyford, Co. Dublin. The Statues of Liberty, Justice and Wisdom on the Westmoreland Street side were also restored.

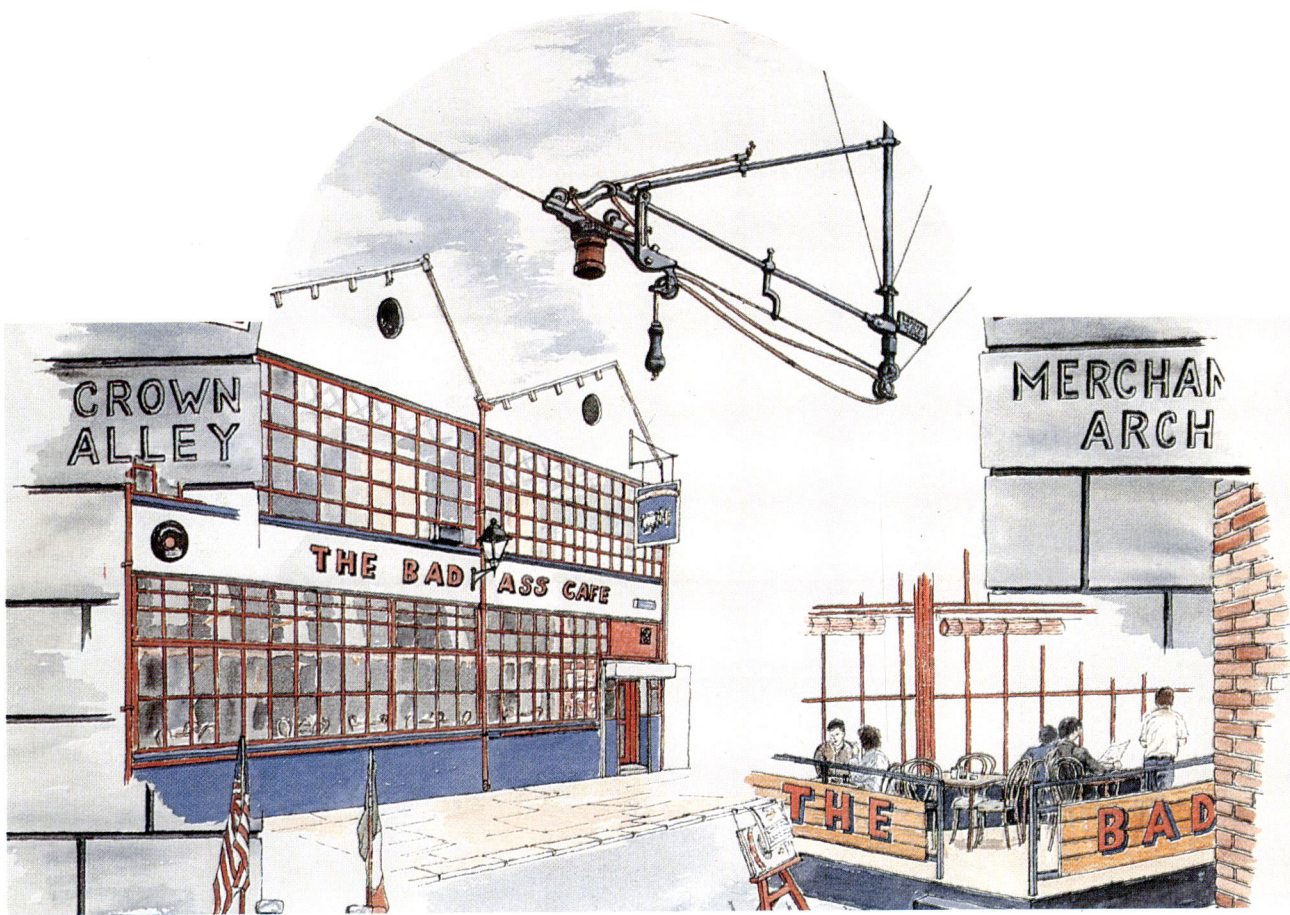

Bad Ass Cafe,
No.9 Crown Alley.

This restaurant, synonymous with Crown Alley for the last decade, is in a successfully converted tea merchant's warehouse. A nice touch inside and reminiscent of a bygone era is the fully working rapid wire system which communicates messages from each table to the kitchen. The exact positioning of the donkey's hoof prints implanted in the footpath outside was determined by walking the cafe's famous mascot over the path which was first covered with sand.

**Webb's Bookshop,
Crampton Quay.**

Crampton Quay was once famous, along with Aston Quay, as a street of booksellers. George Webb's is still a reminder of those days with its secondhand bookstalls encouraging pavement browsing. Webb's has been owned by the well-known bookselling firm of Fred Hanna since the mid 1940's. This shop was a favourite haunt of the Fenian, John O'Leary, who had amassed 10,000 volumes in his private library collection. Famous literary figures such as James Joyce, Oscar Wilde, George Bernard Shaw, W.B. Yeats, Sean O'Casey and Samuel Beckett were known to have perused the volumes on the bookstalls.

A comparison between the Dame Street of the 1790's as depicted by James Malton and that of the 1990's.

Saints Michael and John's Church, Exchange Street Lower.

In 1818 a bell was hung in the belfry of the new church of Saints Michael and John, and its peal was the first sound from a Roman Catholic Church in Ireland for nearly three hundred years. The Penal Laws, although relaxed in practice, were still in force and one Alderman Carlton instituted proceedings to have the bell silenced. Daniel O'Connell took up the defence and on the advice of the Attorney-General the case was dropped. The bell later became the official symbol during the 1929 centenary celebrations of Catholic Emancipation. The bell is still usable but was recast in 1940 to correct a crack.

Built by public donations and by the free labour of Dublin tradesmen, the new church was partially opened on Christmas Day 1813 and completed within the next two years. It was designed by J. Taylor.

The church was named after both Saints Michael and John, the former being the parish for Rosemary Lane and the latter being the parish for the new location. As well as combining these parishes, the church also absorbed the two pre-Reformation parishes of Saints Werburgh and Nicholas within the walls. The church has been closed for worship since the late 1980's.

Michael and John's Church stands on the site of the Smock Alley Theatre (see Essex Street West, page 120).

The large Georgian house standing on its own next to the former church of Saints Michael and John was the presbytery and the buildings on the other side were the parish schools.

Former Music Hall, Fishamble Street.

Very little of the old hall still exists, only a wall foundation or two. Handel's "Messiah" was premiered here in 1742 but the building ceased to be a performance hall in the 1860's when Kennan & Son, Turning Lathe & Tool Manufacturers, acquired the premises.

Kennans, established in 1770, later owned most of the block from the corner of Essex Street West to a few doors beyond the old Music Hall (see also page 35).

In the 1930's Rowntree-Mackintosh moved into Kennan's unwanted space while they were waiting for their new factory to be built on Inchicore Road.

**Old Electrical Power Station,
Fleet Street.**

Dublin Corporation obtained an order from the Board of Trade in 1808 to begin a system to supply electricity to Dublin. Within three years work commenced on the new power station in Fleet Street and on the laying of underground cables. The huge dynamos, engines and 14 feet (4.2 metres) diameter fly-wheels, laid on a 16 feet (4.8 metres) thick bed of reinforced concrete, were installed by Messrs. Hammond & Co. Work was completed and the plant handed over to the Electric Lighting Company of Dublin Corporation on 23rd September 1892. Total cost was £38,000.

The Metropole and Shelbourne Hotels were the first commercial units to be supplied with the new incandescent lights and street lighting was installed along Grafton, College, Dame, Parliament, Capel, Mary, Henry, Sackville (O'Connell), D'Olier, Westmoreland Streets and College Green using 78 lamp posts.

The 900 kilowatts were produced by a staff of one manager, one electrician, one switchroom attendant, three drivers, three dynamomen, two cleaners, one fitter, three lamp trimmers and two boilermen.

The new venture was so successful that in the space of a year an extension was built and by 1903 the power station was relocated to Pigeon House Fort on the River Liffey estuary. Fleet Street was then used as the central distribution station for the system.

The Electricity Supply Board (ESB) was established in 1927 and a new switching station and control centre was opened in Bedford Row.

The next major development in Fleet Street for the ESB was the opening in 1957/58 of the shop and offices building located nearer Westmoreland Street.

Its original functions abandoned, the old redbricked power station has served in the last few decades as a transport garage for the ESB and is now set to be revitalised for new uses.

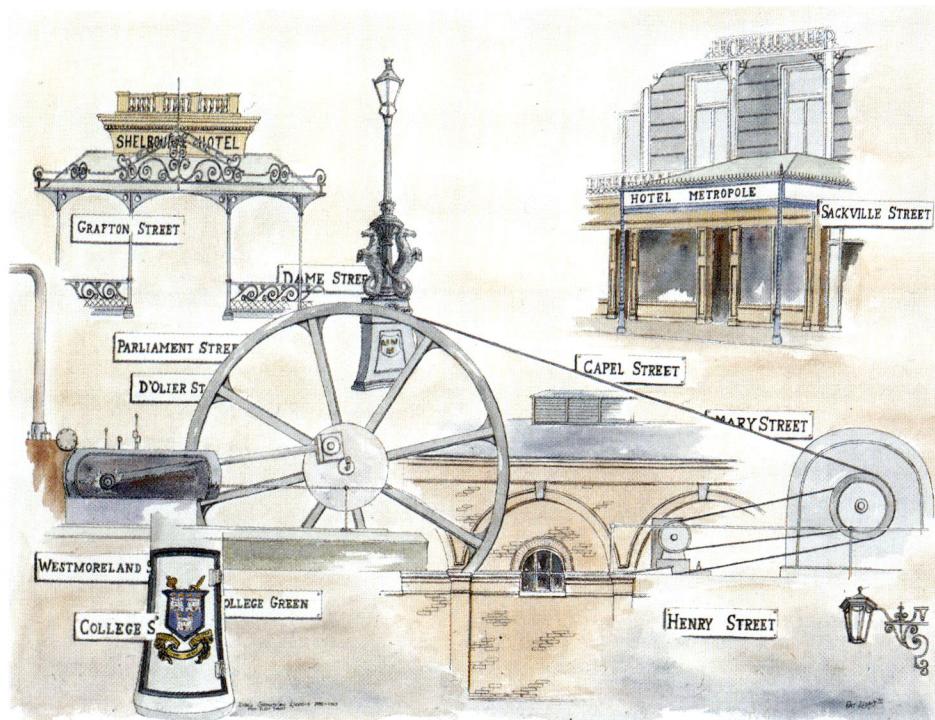

Old Electrical Power Station, Fleet Street.
Montage depicting one of the electrical generators in the Fleet Street power-house and the places and buildings first lit from there in 1892.

No.26 Fishamble Street

As it stands now this house dates from the 1720's but it is known that it was built on much earlier foundations and that its predecessor might have been a wooden framed house. This would make it probably the longest inhabited family dwelling in the city centre.

The adjoining house was demolished in 1986 and after that it was necessary to shore up the corner house. This end of Lower Exchange Street, where the house is presently entered from, was widened in the last decade when the opposite corner property was taken away.

Armoury, Bank of Ireland.

Once the Old Guard House of the Bank of Ireland, the classical facade of the building closing off Foster Place is surmounted by a trophy of arms and armour executed by Joseph R. Kirk. After 1922 this building housed the offices of the Currency Commission and later the Central Bank until it changed premises in 1978.

Sensitive refurbishment has since been carried out by the Bank of Ireland who have turned it into an Arts Centre.

McKeever & Son, Solicitors, Foster Place.

The two adjoining houses at the end of the street appear much as all six of the houses would have looked two hundred years ago. They are now occupied by McKeever & Son, Solicitors. Once the residence of officials of the Parliament, No. 5 had an underground passage to the Parliament House which has long since been blocked up. Until 1986 there was a right-of-way through No. 6 for members of the Stock Exchange in Anglesea Street.

McKeever's was founded in Drogheda in 1898, moved to Dublin in 1926 and has been in Foster Place since 1930.

O'Reilly's Fine Art Auction Rooms, Upper Exchange Street.

A long-established family firm of fine art valuers and estate agents, this firm occupies the former dispatch rooms and offices of the defunct Dublin "Evening Mail" newspaper. Co-incidentally the firm of Michael Reilly & Co., grocers and spirit dealers, traded from here in 1846.

Merchants' Hall, Crampton Quay.

The Merchants' Guild leased a plot of ground from the Wide Streets Commissioners in 1821 and by the next year had their new hall built at a cost of £2,482. Among the city's twenty five historic guilds the Merchants' Guild (also known as the Fraternity of the Holy Trinity) was ranked first. The Guild rode next to the Lord Mayor and the City Council as they traversed the city's boundaries when "Riding the Franchises". In the eighteenth century the merchants displayed their wealth and power when they commissioned the building of the Royal Exchange (City Hall). The Guild became defunct after the Municipal Corporation Reform Act of 1840 which curbed the political privileges of the Guilds.

The Hall was then occupied by a succession of merchants, traders, an evangelical group (The Dublin City Mission), the Merchant Tailor's School (1873 — 1908), Richard Atkinson, poplin manufacturers (1910-1949) and Noonan Shirt Manufacturer (1949-1980).

Architect was Frederick Darley (1798-1870) for which he received the sum of £101, equivalent to about one third of the commission architects usually receive today.

Sunlight Chambers was built at the turn of the century and replaced a number of shops, including the premises of Mason Instruments (established in 1813 and still trading elsewhere in the city).

It was built by Lord Leverhulme of Lever Brothers as his Irish head-office. This period saw a great awakening in sanitation awareness and the soap bar became ubiquitous. The trade name was Sunlight, hence the name Sunlight Chambers.

As part of their education and advertising programme the soap company decided to commission a series of panels placed over the ground and first floor windows, depicting the story of soap. These friezes were sculpted in terracotta and coloured. They illustrate the extraction of raw material for soap, merchants buying and selling oils, and manufacturing processes. The everyday use of soap is represented by women using scrubbing boards and visiting washing rooms. Four of the panels remain unfinished.

The building is presently owned by a firm of solicitors.

Sunlight Chambers, Parliament Street.

A view from the north side of the River Liffey looking up Parliament Street as depicted by James Malton in the 1790's compared to the same view today.

Bewley's Cafe, Westmoreland Street.

In the early 1840's Joshua Bewley arrived from England and opened his small tea & coffee shop in Sycamore Alley, beside the Olympia Theatre.

In due course the first of the three famous city centre shops, 13 South Great George's Street, was opened. Initially coffee was sold only in small quantities and, to encourage sales, coffee making demonstrations were held at the back of the shop. Home-made rolls were served with the coffee and thus began the cafes and the bakery.

In 1916 the second shop, in Westmoreland Street, was opened.

Known at one time as Bewley's Oriental Cafes, the "Oriental" part of the name was dropped in 1972 as Far Eastern vases and ornaments had not been sold by the firm since the outbreak of the Second World War .

In November 1986, after nearly one hundred and fifty years in the Bewley Family, the company was sold to Patrick Campbell of Campbell Catering who turned around the ailing fortunes of the cafes and has even begun to open branches in places as far away as Tokyo, Japan.

The heavily wooded interiors, the old wooden chairs, the aroma of coffee, the fires burning in the ornate fireplaces, the private nooks and the conversations all add to the ambiance that is Bewley's. Unfortunately, a near disastrous fire in the Westmoreland Street branch in 1977 all but destroyed the 19th century interior but rehabilitation has since restored the right atmosphere.

Coffee was first cultivated in Arabia in the 15th century spreading over the entire Arab world. It arrived in Europe via Venice in 1615. The first coffee house in England started up in Oxford in 1650 and shortly afterwards the idea became popular in Dublin. Coffee houses were soon seen as an alternative to taverns especially for gentlemen and merchants discussing business.

Indecon House, Wellington Quay.

Recently restored by owners Gray, Murray and Associates, this house leads directly to its restored other half which faces on to Essex Street East. After Wellington Quay was built, several businesses on Essex Street simply bought plots at their rear and traded in concert or in preference on the new quay.

In 1902 James Joyce sent a postcard (still extant) from Paris to John F. Byrne who was living at 20 Essex Street East, the back-to-back dwelling with Indecon House. On the postcard was a poem reflecting, "On the journeyings of the soul". John F. Byrne had been a student friend of Joyce in his university days and the writer based the character Cranly in the "Portrait of the Artist" on him.

Mulvany Brothers, Wellington Quay.

The Mulvany family have been in the picture framing business since 1881 but are only in these premises since 1961. Picture restoration and gilding are also specialities of the firm.

Previous occupants of the shop were Stenor's Vulcanising Machines (from 1940–61) and Peter Ceppi and Sons, also picture framers and in business from the 1870s.

In 1932 the offices of the Eucharistic Congress were on the second floor.

DAME STREET
(North side)

Origin of name: After the Church of Mary del Dam built in 1385. The dedication of the Church in turn probably derived from a dam for a mill-race on the Poddle nearby.

Irish name: Sráid an Dáma.

Former names: Teyngmouth or Thingmote Street (after the Viking ceremonial mound at present-day Trinity Street) and Damas or Damask Street, named Dame Street circa 1600.

Laid down: Originally a track laid down in the 12th century to serve a number of religious institutions situated to the East of the city walls.

Development: Dame Street was one of the first tentative excursions outside of the City Walls. Starting from the old Dame's Gate, the main eastern gate of the city (near the present-day Olympia), slowly developed, first as a narrow lane and then as a more confident street after the opening of Trinity College in 1592. Dame's Gate was demolished in 1698. An outer defence gate, known as the Blind Gate, had been erected at the eastern end of the early Dame Street.

Although a considerable part of the street had already been built by the early 1700's, houses were demolished in 1769 by the Wide Streets Commissioners to widen the street. In the 19th century, Dame Street, along with College Green, established itself as the insurance, banking and commercial centre of Dublin with very fine examples of Victorian architecture. Nevertheless small trades were also represented, for example, by the many tailoring firms setting up here. Dame Street is now well furnished with French, Italian and Chinese restaurants and a number of pubs.

Sign of the Times

About Ten O'Clock at Night some Rogues broke a Pane of Glass in the Bar of the Turk's-Head Tavern on Temple Bar, and carried off Three silver punch Ladles.

The Freeman's Journal 28 — 31 March 1767.

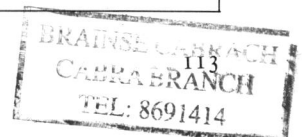

A Ruffian called William Ross, otherwise Bill the Tripper, armed with a Cutlas, was sent to Newgate last Night by Sheriff Lightburne. He may be viewed by any Persons that have been stopped lately in the Streets.

The Freeman's Journal 28 — 31 March 1767.

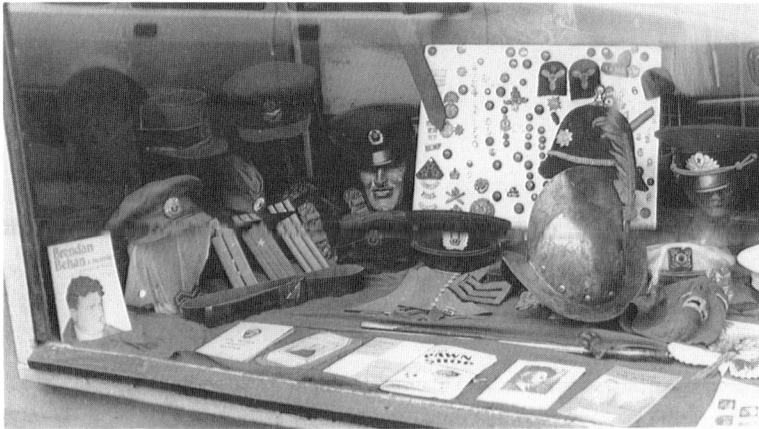

P.J. Bourke's, Dame Street.

The founder of this firm of theatrical costumiers, Patrick J. Bourke, was part lessee of the Queen's Theatre from 1928 when the partnership of Ireland's most famous comedians of the time, Jimmy O'Dea and Harry O'Donovan, first blossomed.

Bourke's costume business started in 1934 and it has since dressed countless stage and film productions.

Patrick Bourke, himself a prolific playwrite, wrote and part-directed the first full length Irish film "Ireland a Nation" in 1913. When it was first shown in 1917 three British Army armoured cars arrived outside the Rotunda Cinema and seized the film.

"Crann an Óir" (Tree of gold), Central Bank, Dame Street.
Sculptor: Eamonn O'Doherty.

Riverrun Gallery, Dame Street.

114

ESSEX GATE

Origin of name: See Essex Street East, page 117.

Irish name: Geata Essex.

Date laid down: 1675.

Development: This very short winding street was built on the site of Buttevant's Tower, one of the medieval city's strong points, to help ease the town's traffic congestion!

Rapid expansion of the city in the mid 1600's swept away what would now be regarded as precious architectural heritage. Buttevant's Tower was demolished in the 1670's and replaced by Essex Gate connecting Essex Street West with its eastern counterpart.

The street directories list only one commercial premises in 1762 and three in 1846 — a cork cutter, a merchant and Lundy Foot & Co., tobacco and snuff manufacturers.

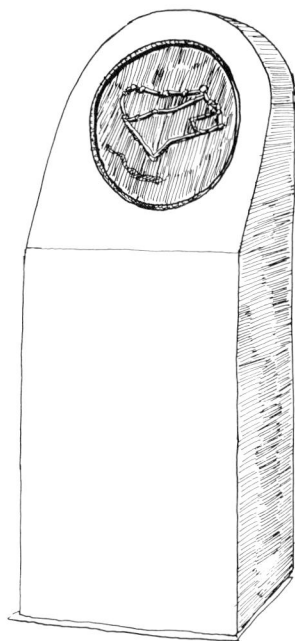

Towers and Gates site markers.
These plaques, erected all around the perimeter of the medieval walled city show where each tower and gate once stood.

Cathair Books, Essex Gate.

A bookshop very much in the time-honoured tradition of being willing to trace any book, from new to antiquarian, for its customers.

ESSEX QUAY

Origin of name: From the Earl of Essex but more likely named after the 1676 Essex Bridge.

Irish name: Cé Essex.

Date laid down: There was probably a timber slipway here until a proper quay was built of stone in the late 1600's.

Development: This was the most eastern riverfront just outside the medieval wall which ran along Blind Quay (Lower Exchange Street). The quay was used along with Wood Quay until port facilities moved further down river in the late 17th century. Sir Patrick Dun's hospital was founded on Essex Quay under the will of Dun, a Scottish doctor, but was moved in 1808 to Grand Canal Street.

The curved inset in the footpath as it approaches Fishamble Street is a relatively recent amendment as the pavement line of Essex Quay used to be much nearer to the river wall. This allowed the presence of a whole row of houses that are now gone and where building in the future would be difficult due to the narrow site. In 1850 no less than thirty one traders sold their wares from Essex Quay.

Situated at the Eastern end of the quay was Isolde's Tower, a massive keep over forty foot (12.2 metres) high.

"Baite", Essex Quay.
Sculpture of a Viking Ship entitled "Baite" by Betty Maguire located on Essex Quay. The sculpture was commissioned in 1988 by the Sculptors' Society of Ireland in co-operation with Dublin Corporation and An Foras Áiseanna Saothair (FÁS) for Dublin's Millennium.

ESSEX STREET EAST

Origin of name: Arthur Capel, Earl of Essex, Lord Lieutenant 1672-1677.

Irish name: Sráid Essex Thoir.

Date laid down: From about 1620 when reclamation took place in order to build the Custom House.

Development: Fashionable new houses sprang up along Essex Street East with the development of Custom House Quay. Several of them had overhanging summer houses (which would be like conservatories today) built on the river side so that residents could enjoy the river and its traffic.

One famous institution was the Globe Coffee House frequented by merchants of all sorts. Other coffee houses also traded along the street.

Rathborne Wax Chandlers had their base here in the 1740's (see Crampton Court, page 91).

A well known resident of Essex Street East was George Faulkner (1699-1775) who founded his printing works on the same street. He was Dean Jonathan Swift's publisher and in 1725 he launched the "Dublin Journal".

First published in 1689 by James II and suppressed a year later by William of Orange, the official government periodical, the "Dublin Gazette" was relaunched in 1705 at the Custom House Printing house on Essex Street East. It has been continuously published since then although the name changed to "Iris Oifigiúil" in this century.

Dolphin House, Essex Street East.

The Victorian splendour of the former Dolphin Hotel was designed by J. J. O'Callaghan and built 1896 — 1898. The hotel enjoyed a reputation, especially among the racing fraternity, for its wholesome steak and fish menus.

It was founded by Michael Nugent, a wine and spirit merchant (see page 47). Business declined in the 1970's and the hotel was gone by 1979. The elaborate interior was gutted before conversion for use by the Dublin Metropolitan District Court.

The Project Arts Centre,
39 Essex Street East.

The Project Arts Centre was founded as an Artists'
Collective in 1967 in Lower Abbey Street and
moved twice after that before arriving at its current
home, the former Dollard Printing house, in 1974.
Founded as an avant-garde organisation, it has and
still continues to provide a challenging alternative
entry into the world of dramatic and musical performance and the visual arts.

The accommodation on Essex Street East
includes a gallery, a theatre and workshop space.
An earlier cinema was destroyed by a fire in the
1980's.

The Project was the first cultural pioneer to
move into the area in the latter half of this century.

Bad Bob's,
Essex Street East.

This grandiose establishment
did not start life as a pub but
was designed for an allied
trade, Michael Nugent's
Wine & Spirit Merchants.
The Nugents also owned the
Dolphin Hotel at the corner
with Crane Lane.

No.20 Essex Street East

John F. Byrne, who lived at No.20 was a personal friend of James Joyce's and was the character on whom Cranley was based in "Portrait of the Artist".

Across the road, at the corner with Eustace Street, is the Norseman Public House keeping up a tradition in wines and spirits offered from these premises for over one hundred and fifty years.

Essex Street East.
View of Essex Street looking East, showing the curve riverwards in the road after it had passed the Old Custom House.

119

ESSEX STREET WEST

Origin of name: Earl of Essex.

Irish name: Sráid Essex Thiar.

Former names: As might be expected the narrow streets within the medieval walls were renamed several times. Essex Street West was known as Stable Lane (1646), Cadogan's Alley (1659), Smock (or Smoke) Alley (1661), Orange Street (1724) and finally its present name (1840).

Laid down: The street is not shown as such on John Speed's map of 1610, so even though the streets around it date further back by several hundred years it must be assumed that the development of Essex Street West did not begin until perhaps the 1620's or later. 1633 is a date selected by Leonard R. Strangeways in his map of 1904.

Development: Judging by its former names and the fact that it was wedged in as it was by Blind Quay (Exchange Street Lower), it was probably an inconsequential side alley. Its main claim to fame was the celebrated Smock Alley Theatre which stood where Saints Michael & John's Church was later erected.

Dublin's first theatre opened in Werburgh Street in 1637. In 1661 John Ogilby built Dublin's most famous theatre in Smock Alley. A succession of flamboyant and dedicated managers, a company of famous performers including the renowned Peg Woffington and riotous behaviour of 18th century audiences insured the far flung reputation of the Smock Alley Playhouse. It had its fair share of disasters too. In 1671 the galleries fell down killing three people and again more died in 1701 as a result of a row. In 1754 rioters tore the place to pieces. Final curtain call came in 1790. The building was demolished in 1815 but it is thought that the burial vaults in the church of Saints Michael & John originally formed the pit of the playhouse.

Smock Alley Theatre.

Until the 1940's when it was partially widened, the street followed its more ancient curved narrow pattern. At the same time as the widening of the street, the two and three storey Georgian period houses and the stables of Kennan's Ironworks on the south side of Essex Street West were razed to the ground.

30th Anniversary Performance

**For the Benefit of the Lying-In Hospital,
At the Theatre in Smock-alley,
This present Evening, Thursday April 16, 1772,**

**The Sacred ORATORIO of the MESSIAH
Composed by Handel.**

Will be performed under the Direction of Mr. Barthelemon. The principal vocal Parts by Signor Fedele, Mr. Passerini, Mr. Wann, and Mrs. Barthelemon.

Between the first and second Acts will be performed, an Organ Concerto by Mr. Mahernbolty, a celebrated Performer just arrived from Germany, who is blind; and between the second and third Acts, a Concerto for Violin by Mr. Barthelemon.
Places in the Boxes to be taken of Mr. Kane at the Theatre from Eleven o'Clock to Three.
Boxes and Lattices 5s.5d. Pit 3s.3d. Middle Gallery 2s.2d
Upper Gallery 1s.1d.
Subscribers Tickets for the twelfth and last Concerts will be admitted to any part of the House.
To begin at seven o'Clock.

N.B. The House will be illuminated with Wax, with great Additions and Improvements.

The Freeman's Journal 14-16 April 1772.

THEATRICAL INTELLIGENCE

His Excellency the Lord Lieutenant will honour the Theatre Royal in Smock-Alley, with his presence this evening, to see the Italian Comic Opera of La Fraschetana.

ITALIAN OPERA

To prevent Inconvenience to the Nobility and Gentry in getting to their Carriages, they are respectfully entreated to give positive Orders to their Servants, to set down with their Horses Heads towards Essex-street.

N.B. The old Pit Door will be opened every Night for Chairs only.

The Freeman's Journal 11 — 13 January 1777.

By Permission of the Right Hon. the Lord Mayor.

THEATRE ROYAL, SMOCK ALLEY

By his Majesty's Servants.

**On Saturday next, will be performed an Italian comic OPERA, called
LA FRASCHETANA**

First Violin Signor Georgi.

The Harpsichord by Signor St. George.

Boxes and Pit 7s. 6d. English, Middle Gall. 3s English, Upper Gall. 2s. English.

By Order of the Committee no Person will be allowed to keep Places in the Galleries.

N.B. NO Money whatsoever will be returned at any of the Doors.

The Theatre is perfectly well aired, Stoves having been placed in different Parts of the House for that Purpose, and will be continued on the Day of Representation.

The Freeman's Journal 2 — 4 December 1777.

TO BE LET

For any term that may be agreed on, or the Interest of the Leases to be held, the extensive Building the THEATRE-ROYAL, SMOCK ALLEY, together with the adjoining Dwelling-house, to which there are the most commodious Vaults of any house in Dublin; the Theatre subject to the small yearly rent of 60L. per annum, the Dwelling-house to 28L. 8s. 9d. — also to rent the House in TEMPLE-LANE, lately known by the name of the Shakespeare Tavern, adjoining in Crow-street. From the central situation of the above tenements it is needless to say more, than that they are all remarkably well calculated for any persons in the Mercantile or Public Business — application to be made to R. Daly, Esq. only, No. 10 Harcourt Street, Dublin.

The Freeman's Journal 11 — 13 December 1787.

**At the THEATRE in SMOCK-ALLEY
For the BENEFIT of the MEATH HOSPITAL
On Friday the 10th of April will be performed the Tragedy**

B A R B A R O S S A

Zaphira, by Mrs. Fitzhenry, being the only time she will perform this Season.

Tickets to be had at Alderman George Faulkner's the Bar of the Exchange Coffee-house, and Meath Hospital in Earl-street.

It is hoped there will be no Drum or Party on the above Night to the Prejudice of this useful Charity.

The Freeman's Journal 31 Mar — 2 April 1772.

EUSTACE STREET

Origin of name: From Sir Maurice Eustace, speaker of the House of Commons (1639) and Lord Chancellor (1644). His residence and gardens stood on the site before development took place. Eustace was, with the Duke of Ormonde, responsible for the creation of the wall in the Phoenix Park. He died in 1665 from his exertions and the ill health he had sustained earlier in England when he had been imprisoned for supporting Charles II.

Irish name: Sráid Iústas.

Date laid down: Between 1680 — 1720 as "the intended street from Damask (Dame) Street to Temple Bar".

Development: Originally this was a tidal shore where the River Poddle flowed into the Liffey which in the early 1600's was reclaimed by Jacob Newman.

The street developed primarily as a merchant centre but was liberally peppered with taverns with fine sounding names; the "Eagle" (1712), the "Punch Bowl" (1727), the "Three Stags Heads" (1754) and the "Ship" (1758).

Into this world of commerce and revelry there arrived some strange bedfellows. In 1705 the Quakers extended from Sycamore Alley into Eustace Street and in 1728 the Presbyterian congregation moved down from New Street.

To collect new taxes imposed in 1773 the Stamp Office of Ireland was housed at No. 5 Eustace Street, next door to the residence of George Cleghorn, an eminent military surgeon of his day.

Liptons, at one time a household name in the grocery trade, had its principal shop at Nos 1 & 2 at the corner with Dame Street.

There are still some examples of early Georgian houses on Eustace Street with original interior features such as fine staircases and plaster work.

Eustace Street, 1910.

SAINT WINIFRED'S WELL

The following text is taken from the wall plaque erected next to the well.

"This well was probably constructed when Eustace Street was laid out between 1680 and 1720. Before that this area was a salty tidal shore on the right bank of the river Poddle where it joined the Liffey just outside the walls of medieval Dublin.

Embankments were built in the early 17th century and this allowed the shore to be reclaimed. Fresh groundwater flowed in behind the embankment and flushed the salts out of the old beach deposits.

Water supply must have been a problem for the first inhabitants of Eustace Street so the well was dug to draw upon the groundwater flowing gently from the South beneath the street. It provided a supply for the local residents, stabled animals and street traders. The absence of rope marks on the stone lining suggests that the water was drawn from the well by hand pump.

St. Winifred's Well was a medieval well known to have been in Eustace Street, perhaps further up towards Dame Street. St. Winifred lived in Holywell (North Wales) in the 7th century. She was revered in North Wales in the middle ages and, like St. Brigid in Ireland, her name was associated with wells and springs. It is not clear how a well in medieval Dublin came to bear her name. It is known that Dublin had trading contact with North Wales from the 11th century onwards and settlers from there probably came to live in Dublin after the Anglo-Normans captured the city in 1170. One of these may have given the well its name. The well may have belonged to the Augustinian friary of the Holy Trinity, founded in the 13th century, which was located 50 metres from here (in what is now Cecilia Street).

The present well had been covered over by the street at some point in the past. It has been restored to expose the ground water resource that flows all the time below the foundations of the city. In other parts of the city groundwater is being used for industrial supplies and to heat and cool buildings".

The well, 19 feet (almost 6 metres) to the bottom and up to 8 feet (2.5 metres) of water depth, was rediscovered in 1991 when workmen were laying cobbles on the street.

St. Winifred's Well, Eustace Street.

THE QUAKERS IN DUBLIN

The Religious Society of Friends was introduced into Ireland in 1654. Most of the early adherents came over from Britain with the various waves of Protestant settlers. These Quakers were mainly tradesmen, merchants and farmers.

Down the centuries the Friends took an active role in the commercial and philanthropic life of Ireland and some Quaker families, including those of Pim, Jacob, Bewley, Walpole, Webb and Haughton, became household names in Dublin.

During the Great Hunger of 1846/7 a group of Quakers formed a Central Relief Committee and soup kitchens were opened throughout the country. To help the starving poor to become more self sufficient, the committee also distributed tons of seeds to farmers and grant-aid to fishermen.

The Dublin Quakers, obliged by the Penal Laws not to open any meeting house on a main street, first met in Bride's Alley (beside St. Nicholas Street), moved to Wormwood Gate (near Bridge St), next to Cole's Alley (Meath Street) and finally to Sycamore Alley in 1692.

Number 6 Eustace Street

In 1705 they purchased a plot on the developing Eustace Street and over the next one hundred and fifty years they merged and expanded the buildings between Sycamore and Eustace Streets. About ten years ago the Quakers relinquished Number 6 and moved their meetings next door.

Imaginatively restored and adapted, Number 6 now houses the Irish Film Centre which opened on the 27th September 1992. Contained within are: two cinemas, the Irish Film Archive, ten film organisations, educational and conference facilities and a film library. The design is by architects O'Donnell and Twomey and the main contractors were Cleary and Doyle.

The Former Presbyterian School, Eustace Street.
In 1728 the Presbyterian congregation moved to Eustace Street from New Street.

EXCHANGE STREET UPPER AND LOWER

Origin of name: After the Royal Exchange (City Hall) on Cork Hill.

Irish name: Sráid Iosóilde Uacht & Iocht.
   The Irish name is derived from Isolde's Tower which was a medieval fortification between Lower Exchange Street and Essex Quay.

Former names: The river end was called Blind Quay (because it wasn't actually on the river), the upper end was known as Scarlet Alley, Isod's Lane and Blind Quay Upper. Both sections were renamed Exchange Street Upper and Lower in the 1770's after the opening of the Royal Exchange.

Development: The street led from Wood Quay and was the most direct route for centuries to the Castle. It ran along the inside of the East wall of the fortified town. The curve on Exchange Street Lower follows almost directly the line of the old wall. Its narrowness is typical of medieval streets. Three city towers stood along here, namely; Case's Tower, Isolde's Tower and Buttevant's Tower. Presumably the foundations of both towers and walls are still waiting for excavation.
   A lane once joined Lower Exchange Street to West Essex Street.
   Because of its proximity to the old Custom House small service trades and warehouses were the main occupants until the end of the 18th century. Tobacconists were in the majority, there being no less than five recorded in 1762.

Sign of the Times

DUBLIN LAMP-OFFICE

At JOHN BRAY, No. 21 Fishamble Street, Contractor for Lighting the City of Dublin, under the Right Honourable the Directors and Commissioners for Paving, &c. where Complaints for neglect of Duty in the Lighters, will be thankfully received and immediately attended to.

The Freeman's Journal 22 — 24 November 1787.

At Night ——— Brady, a Constable, seized a Footpad on the Blind-quay, the fellow resisted and drew a Pistol on him; but Brady got him down and wrested the Pistol from him; During the Struggle, an Accomplice came up and with a Slater's Lathing-hammer in his Hand, threatened that if Brady did not let the Fellow escape, he would beat his Brains out. Brady immediately turned the Pistol against the Slater, fired at him and wounded him in the Face and Breast and thus secured the two Villains, who were lodged in Newgate. We submit it to the Public, whether this active and Spirited Peace Officer, be not so far intitled to their countenance and protection, as to procure him a pecuniary reward, which may be easily effected, by a Voluntary Subscription.

The Freeman's Journal 28 — 31 March 1767.

FISHAMBLE STREET
(East Side)

Origin of name: From the Fish Shambles or Stalls.

Irish name: Sráid Sheamlas an Éisc.

Former names: Fish Shambles c 1408 (later found on Speed's Map of 1610).
Vicus Piscariorum (Fishmongers' Quarters) c 1467.
Fish Street c 1470.
Fisher Street c 1570.
Saint Tulloch's Lane (the section from Essex Street to Exchange St. Lower). — A corruption of the name of Saint Olaf King of Norway who died 1030. A church dedicated to him once stood in Fishamble Street. The name dates from the thirteenth century.
Bothe Street (Upper Fishamble Street) c 1435.

Date laid down: During the Viking period c 10th/11th century.

Development: Still locally called the "Hill", the curving nature of the road was designed to allow horse-and-man drawn traffic a slightly easier climb from the river.

The richness of the Viking and medieval history of this street alone would require a volume of its own.

Fishamble Street in the 17th and 18th centuries was a residential street and such personages as Arthur Annesley, Henry Grattan, the poet James Clarence Mangan and James Ussher, one of the first great scholars of Trinity College, were born here.

Sign of the Times

FISHAMBLE-STREET, AUG. 19, 1780.

At the desire of Several Gentlemen, the MUSIC-HALL will be opened on Tuesday evening the 22nd instant, in order to take into serious consideration the important bills now before Parliament, and to determine what measures are neccessary to preserve the Commerce and Constitution of this country from the fatal effects which those bills, if passed into laws, must occasion. It is hoped Merchants, and Volunteers in particular, will attend, being now the properest persons to discuss matters of such moment.

The doors will be opened at six, and a Gentleman called to the chair at seven o'clock.

Admittance 6d. a head.

The Freeman's Journal 19 August 1780.

The General Post Office was situated on the street from 1684 to 1709. The new Music Hall was opened in 1741 and a year later Handel gave the first performance there of the "Messiah" (see page 35). Nine taverns are recorded on the street during the 1760's.

Up to relatively recent times there were several minor streets leading into Fishamble Street that were closed off only a decade or two ago. Until Lord Edward Street was opened in 1886 Fishamble Street ran as far as Castle Street and at the point where the new street meets Fishamble Street, Saul's Court was located. On the western side there were also several alleyways and lanes now gone forever under the Civic Offices.

Interestingly the Wilson's 1762 Street Directory lists twenty eight shops and businesses with as many as five grocers, six apothecaries and five goldsmiths — does this say anything about the lifestyle of the street's residents?

Interior of Fishamble Street Music Hall
(This view dates from a rebuilding after 1742).

Sign of the Times

About Nine o'Clock at Night a man was attacked by a single Foot-pad in Fishamble Street, who robbed him of Five pence and his Pocket Handkerchief.

The Freeman's Journal 26 — 29 December 1767.

FLEET STREET

Origin of name: Like Temple Bar the name partly owes its origin to its namesake in London and to its situation beside the river.

Irish name: Sráid na Tuinne

Laid down: 1660's — 1670's.

Development: The street basically developed with the advantage of College Green on one side and Aston Quay on the other. It was not dissected by Westmoreland Street until 1799.

Fleet Street was a popular location for foreign consuls in the 1800's until most moved out to Eden Quay and then to Ballsbridge. In 1846 the Portugese, Ottoman, Bavarian, Hamburgh, Sardinian and Belgium consuls all kept offices here. In the 1917 street directory (when some of the street lay in ruins after the Rising) there are no less than fifty nine solicitors' firms listed.

Kevin Barry, the youthful patriot who was hanged in Mountjoy Jail in 1920, was born over his father's dairy in Number 8. Numbers 13 — 16 at the corner with Aston Place housed the library of the U.S. Information Service until the 1954 Geneva Conference Agreement closed down all the propaganda outlets of the great powers.

In 1753 a hospital for incurables started in Fleet Street and its successor is now the Royal Hospital, Donnybrook.

Bewley's Chambers, Fleet Street.

Office chambers, let out to small firms like solicitors, were a common feature of late 19th century Dublin.

Solidarity House, Fleet Street.

Now the offices of the Irish Trade Union Trust (offering a range of services to assist both the unemployed and the employed) it was, at the turn of the century, the headquarters of the Irish Women Workers' Union.

FOSTER PLACE

Origin of name: Named after John Foster.

Irish name: Plás Fostar.

Former name: Turnstile Alley.

Date laid down: 1792.

Development: This little gem of a cul-de-sac is passed by tens of thousands of people daily but is hardly ever given a second glance. Yet, to walk over the cobbles up to the former Guard House is like taking a trip back in time to more classical and leisurely days. Foster Place was not always a cul-de-sac. Known as Turnstile Alley from the 1670's, when it was a much narrower thoroughfare, it was connected to Fleet Street. Extensions to the Parliament House in the late 1700's cut it off except for a confined alleyway but this too was closed in 1928 (see Parliament Row). When the western extension of the Parliament building was added in 1787-94, the Wide Streets Commissioners turned narrow Turnstile Lane into Foster Place. Some fine residences, the Hibernian United Services Club, Daly's Club and Lighton's Bank were subsequently erected there.

Right Honourable John Foster (1740 — 1828). Last Speaker of the Irish House of Commons and Chancellor of the Irish Exchequer in 1784.

Sign of the Times

News from Parliament House

Leave is given to bring Heads of a Bill, to encourage the Planting and Preservation of Oak; and Mr Robert French, Mr James Fortescue, and Mr Thomas Dawson, are to prepare and bring in the same.

The Freeman's Journal 26 — 29 December 1767

FOWNES STREET UPPER AND LOWER

Origin of name: From Sir William Fownes, Sheriff of Dublin 1697 and elected Lord Mayor in 1708. Swift described him as a "wise and useful citizen". He was also one of Dublin's wealthiest merchants.

Irish name: Sráid Fobhnais Uacht & Íocht.

Date laid down: Circa 1700.

Development: Initially the street contained some very fine early Georgian residences. Evidence of these with their unusual cut stone window and door surrounds still exist and offer excellent potential for restoration. Because of the proximity of the street to the financial institutions of Dame and College Streets it quickly converted to commercialism. Scriveners, assurance agents, building, investment and loan societies and commission agents rented accommodation here among some other craft professions such as upholders, surgical instrument makers, paper ruler and seal engravers. In 1846, number 19 was the office of Thomas Reynolds, Marshal of Dublin and Registrar of Pawnbrokers in Ireland.

Arthur Griffith (founder of Sinn Fein) had his office in Fownes Street (ironically in a building once owned by John Temple) from where he issued "The United Irishman".

The Scout Shop at number 14 relocated in 1971 from North Frederick Street. The Catholic Boy Scouts of Ireland were formally organised in 1927.

In preparation for the building of the Central Bank the upper end, on the East side of Fownes Street was demolished in the 1970's.

Fownes Street Lower was previously called Bagnio Slip (16th century) where a ferry station was positioned at the slipway. Bagnio equates to brothel which were a main attraction here. Over the years Fownes Street Lower was the scene of many rows and the occasional murder until the slipway was removed to make way for Wellington Quay.

Sign of the Times

About 11 at Night several inoffensive Persons were wounded so dangerously by some Ruffians in Smock-alley, that their Lives are despaired of.

The Freeman's Journal 5 — 8 September 1767.

LORD EDWARD STREET

Origin of name: From Lord Edward Fitzgerald (1763-1798).

Irish name: Sráid an Tiarna Éadbhárd.

Date laid down: Opened 27th July 1886 by Lord Mayor, T.D. Sullivan.

Development: Hard as it might be to imagine now there was no convenient and straight westerly route from Dame Street until Lord Edward Street was opened. Up to then it was necessary to proceed around Cork Hill and up narrow Castle Street.

Part of Cork Hill had to be demolished and a road was driven through houses, yards and lanes until it came out at Skinner's Row (Christ Church Place). The new street revealed a striking fresh vista of Christ Church Cathedral.

Exchange Buildings, now used as Dublin Corporation offices, was formerly the Rover car showrooms. Further up the street is the impressive ruabon brick and terracotta facade of the late Dublin Working Boys' Home and Harding Technical School. Harding was a lady who had bequeathed a large sum of money in her will to the Home. The architect was Albert E. Murray.

It was founded in 1876 by six businessmen who met in St. Anne's Church in Dawson Street to discuss the plight of boys (usually of around 14 years of age) who came from rural Ireland to take up poorly paid apprenticeships in Dublin and who couldn't afford adequate accommodation. Twelve houses were first acquired elsewhere and in 1891 a new building was commissioned in the recently opened Lord Edward Street. It became Ireland's first technical school and had sleeping accommodation for 75 boys.

USIT, the Youth and Student Travel Organisation, bought the old Harding Home in 1987 in order to offer quality budget accommodation in the city centre. USIT carried out extensive refurbishment throughout including restoration of the red terracotta exterior and renamed the building "Kinlay House", in memory of Howard Kinlay, a former president of the Union of Students in Ireland. The splendid Conference Room with its vaulted and beamed ceiling has been named the "Harding Room".

Kinlay House, Lord Edward Street.

132

MERCHANTS' ARCH

Origin of name: Named after Merchants' Hall (see page 108).

Irish name: Áirse Ceannaigh.

Date laid down: 1822.

Development: The Wide Streets Commissioners, when granting the site to the Merchants' Guild, insisted that a right-of-way be allowed from Wellington Quay to Temple Bar. Although agreeing to this the Guild had some misgivings "apprehensive that the public passage from the Quay to Temple Bar under the intended hall will probably become a place liable to various nuisances and instances of immorality in the night time". They suggested the erection of iron gates to be locked at 11 o'clock every night. Their request was curtly rejected by the Commissioners.

Small shops opened and closed down with great regularity at the Temple Bar end of the passageway. At the turn of the century some secondhand bookstores were in place. James Joyce was familiar with the place and had the "Ulysses" character Leopold Bloom buy a copy of "The Sweets of Sin" for his wife Molly from one of the bookstalls.

Thomas Traynor had a shoemakers shop in Merchants' Arch. He fought in the 1916 Rising and was executed by the British during the Black and Tan period.

Earlier this century Lennon's of Merchants' Arch sold secondhand metal goods, safes, cash registers etc.. A story goes that a buyer of one of his safes locked the key into the safe and Lennon was urgently summoned (he could turn his hand to locksmithing). The client was in Dundalk and the fee of £20 was agreed. Lennon duly arrived, opened the safe in no time, whereupon the client, dismayed at how apparently easy it seemed, protested at the £20 fee and refused to pay so much for so little exertion on Lennon's part. Swiftly Lennon locked the safe again with the key still inside and headed back to the train. The client, realising his gaffe, entreated with Lennon, who only agreed to return to his chastened client on a doubling of the fee. The client learned that you pay for years of experience, not just for the moment of execution.

Today, Merchants' Arch is one of the busiest pedestrian routes in the city.

Merchants' Arch.

PARLIAMENT ROW

Origin of name: From the House of Parliament.

Irish name: Rae na Feise.

Former name: Turnstile Alley.

Date laid down: Mid 1600's and renamed Parliament Row circa 1775.

Development: Now a cul-de-sac ending at the rear of the Bank of Ireland this passageway once continued all the way to College Green. The building of the Bank Armoury all but closed it off and it was finally blocked in 1928.

Sign of the Times

GENERAL POST-OFFICE, FOWNES COURT.

Dublin, Oct 3rd. 1777

Whereas it has been discovered in this Office, that Thomas Hopkins Harvey, sworn Assistant to Hannah Harvey, of Gorey, in the County of Wexford, has for some Time past been guilty of many Frauds in the opening of Letters, and stealing thereout Bank Notes, Bills of Exchange, and other Things of Value — AND WHEREAS the said Thomas Hopkins Harvey has absconded Notice is hereby given that a Reward of FIFTY POUNDS Sterling will be paid to any Person or Persons who shall apprehend and lodge the said Thomas Hopkins-Harvey in any of his Majesty's Jails in this Kingdom.

By Order of the Deputy Post-Master General

N.B. The said Thomas Hopkins Harvey is about twenty Years of Age, five Feet Six or Seven Inches, high, full-faced, dark Eyes, and full Eyebrows, his Nose rather flat; wore his own Hair, which is very dark, and curls in on his Neck, generally wore a light blue Coat with a black Cape.

The Freeman's Journal 14 — 16 Oct 1777.

SHAKESPEARE

New Tavern and Chop House

RICHARD LOUGHLIN, (formerally of the King's Arms Tavern, Smock-alley) begs leave to inform his Friends and the Public, that he hath fitted up, in the best manner, the large house in Temple-Lane, Essex-Street, where the late Spranger Barry, Esq. lived, now known by the Sheakespeare Tavern; and where he humbly entreats a continuance of the favour and countenance he amply experienced, and of which he retains the most grateful rememberance.

The Freeman's Journal 6 — 9 November 1784.

The Celebrated
IRISH
WOOLLEN

WAREHOUSE

DILLON

15   14   13   12   11   10   9   8   7   6   5   4   3   2   1

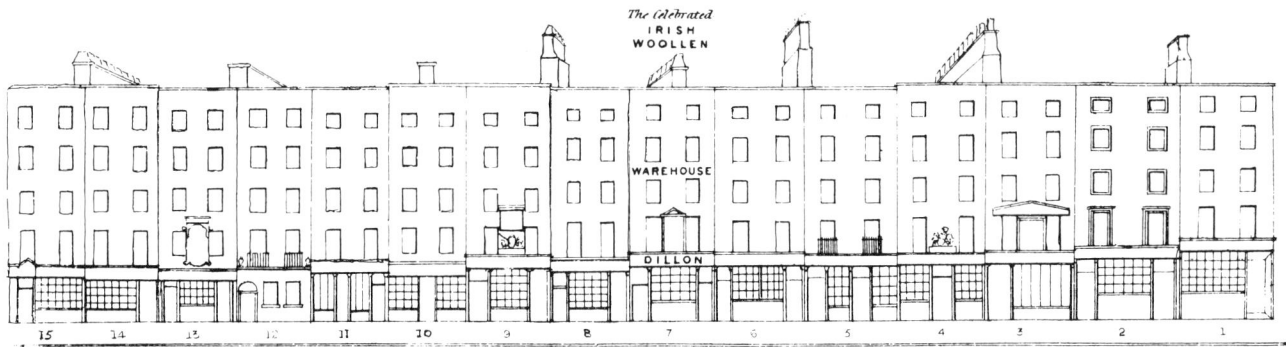

P A R L I A M E N T   S T R E E T

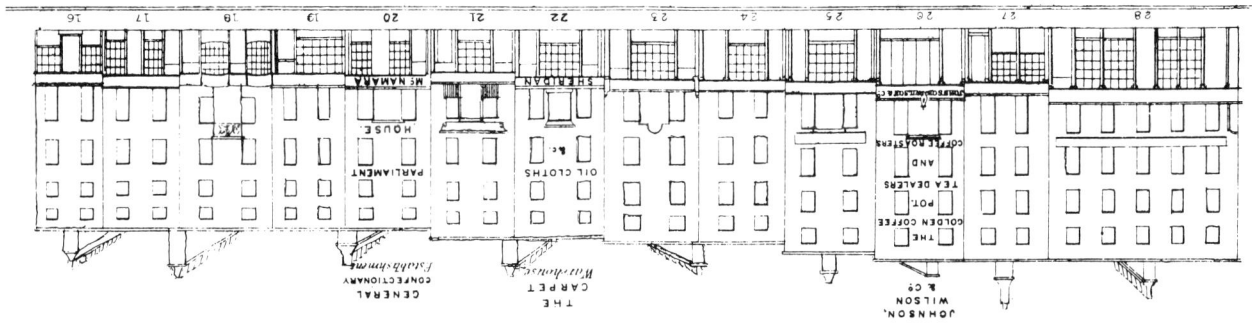

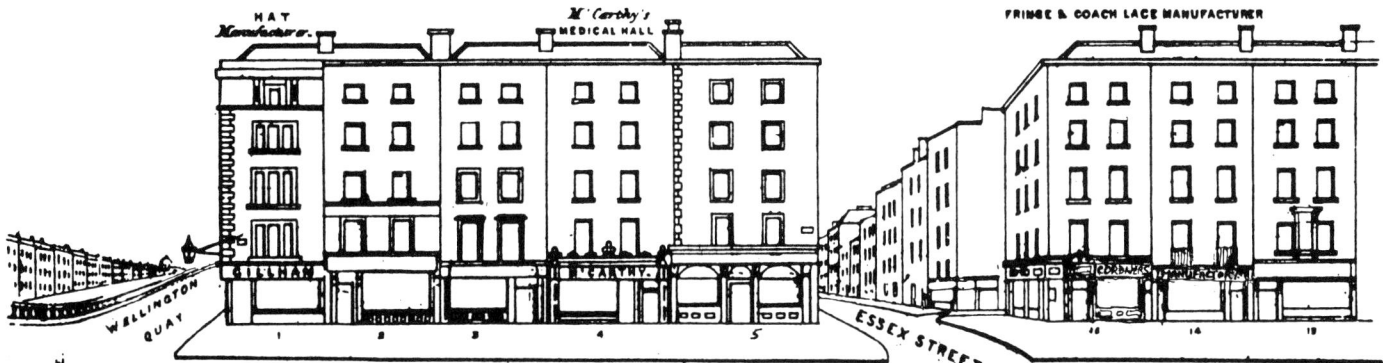

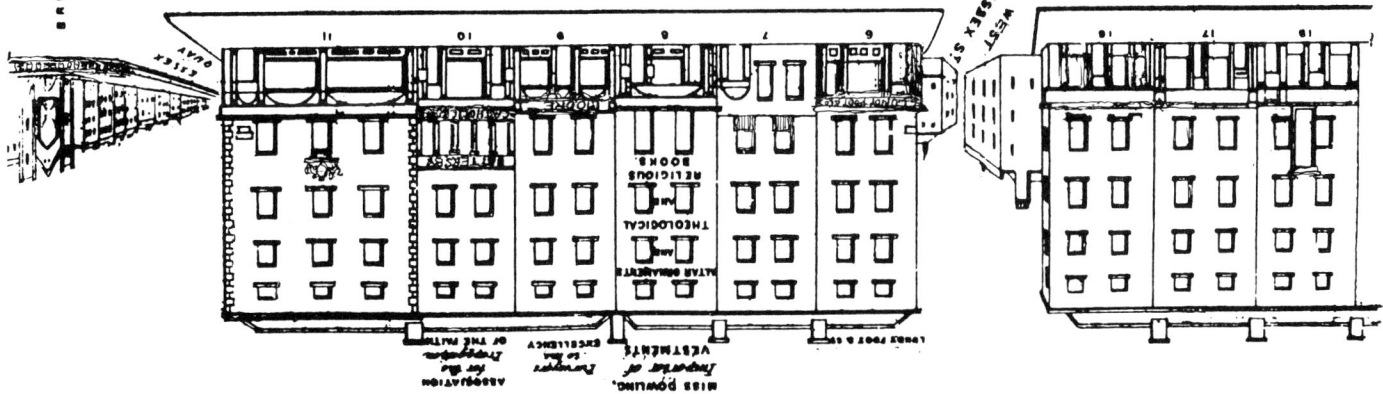

16   17   18   19   20   21   22   23   24   25   26   27   28

Mc NAMARA   SHERIDAN

HOUSE: &c.   COFFEE ROASTERS

PARLIAMENT   OIL CLOTHS   AND   TEA DEALERS

POT,   GOLDEN COFFEE

THE

GENERAL   THE   JOHNSON,
CONFECTIONARY   CARPET   WILSON
Establishment   Warehouse   & Co

HAT   Mc Carthy's   FRINGE & COACH LACE MANUFACTURER
Manufacturer   MEDICAL HALL

GILLMAN   Mc CARTHY'S

WELLINGTON   QUAY   1   2   3   4   5   ESSEX STREET   16   14   15

BRIDGE   E S S E X   B R I D G E   WEST ESSEX ST   PARLIAMENT STREET

ESSEX QUAY   11   10   9   8   7   6

BOOKS   RELIGIOUS

THEOLOGICAL

ALTAR ORNAMENTS   AND

VESTMENTS

MISS DOWLING,
Importer of   EXCELLENCY   by   THE MAT
ASSOCIATION

135

PARLIAMENT STREET

Origin of name: Commemorating a Statute of Parliament of 1757 granting £12,000 to purchase, for the making of the street, the houses that lay in the way between Dame Street and Essex Street. Until 1887 the lower, river end of the street was called Essex Bridge.

Irish name: Sráid na Feise.

Date laid down: 1757 — 1762.

Development: Prior to 1757 the route from Essex Bridge to the Castle or the House of Parliament was through winding narrow streets and the making of this street was the first of the grand visionary plans of the Wide Streets Commissioners to reform the medieval layout of Dublin. However, the eventual destruction of the houses which stood in the way along this proposed route did seriously discommode tenants, many of whom were left without shelter or accommodation (their landlords were of course compensated).

When the street was finished the splendour and elegance of its shops were compared favourably with the best in London. The buildings were built to a common standard; four floors over shop.

Parliament Street, like several other streets, fell on hard times while it struggled to find a new relevance but it is now making a comeback. For instance, the empty Exchange Hotel (one time a temperance or non-alcoholic hotel) has been rehabilitated as an apartment block for inner city living. Some other buildings with 19th century facades have 18th century interiors and have great potential for preservation.

The building on the corner of Parliament Street and Essex Gate stands on the probable site of Buttevant's Tower, a medieval city tower.

Curiously, although Parliament Street led right up to Dublin Castle, the seat of British power before 1922, several clandestine or proscribed political and rebel organisations operated from here. For instance, No. 12 was the address of the Fenian newspaper, the "Irish People".

Number 27 at the South-West corner of Essex Gate was the house of George Faulkner the printer of "The Dublin Journal" (established 1724).

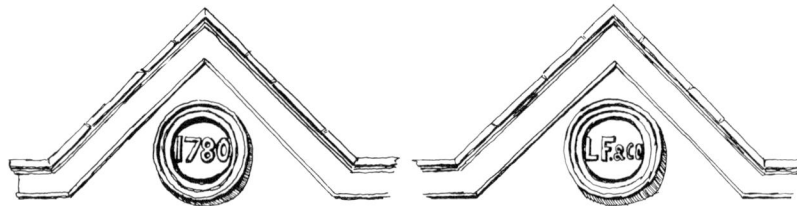

Monogram and date of Lundy Foot & Co.
Apex of building, Parliament Street.
Manufacturers of "Bristol Roll Tobacco", Common Roll, High and Low Scotch Snuff and Superfine Pigtail for Ladies.
Lundy Foot himself was a Lord Mayor of Dublin.

PRICE'S LANE

Origin of name: Untraced (by this author).

Irish name: Lána an Phrísigh.

Date laid down: From at least 1728.

Development: In the 19th century only stables and tenements are recorded as being in Price's Lane including the stables and sheds for the fire engines of the Royal Assurance Company. The lane also provides the rear access to Bewley's and the former McBirney's.

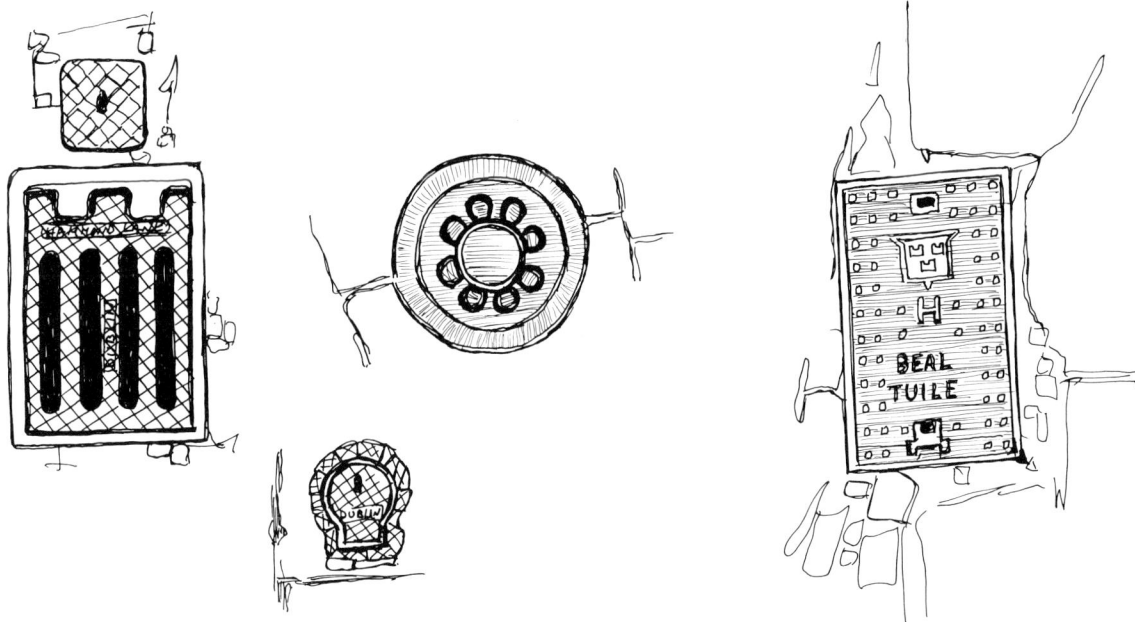

Some examples of manhole covers which can be found throughout Temple Bar.

Sign of the Times

SYCAMORE STREET

Origin of name: Takes its name from the Sycamore tree.

Irish name: Sráid Seiceamair.

Former name: Sycamore Alley (until 1869).

Date laid down: From at least 1728.

Development: The street approximately follows the eastern bank of the now underground River Poddle and proper development of this area only followed when the Liffey/Poddle estuary was reclaimed and built over in the early 1600's.

As with many of the adjoining streets Sycamore Alley developed into a street of taverns, printing houses, storage yards and private residences.

Around 1709, as part of its seemingly endless peregrination until it arrived finally into Sackville (O'Connell) Street, the General Post Office settled for a while in Sycamore Alley. The Post Master General was Isaac Manley, a friend of Swift. At that time the post was delivered only twice a week and often even this schedule was not attained. The G.P.O. moved to Fownes Court (site of the Central Bank) in 1755.

In 1692 the Society of Friends erected a large meeting house which was rebuilt in the following century. The building could also be accessed from Eustace Street.

The most significant event to take place in Sycamore Alley, (from a present-day Dubliners' point of view) was the opening in 1846 in nos. 19 and 20 of Joshua Bewley's first coffee house (see page 111).

In 1883, while the Invincibles had a last drink in the City Hall Inn before setting out on their grisly errand to assassinate Burke and Cavendish in the Phoenix Park, their driver, Skin the Goat, parked his horse and car in Sycamore Street to anxiously await their departure.

Most of the western side of Sycamore Street is taken up by the Olympia Theatre. At the back of the Olympia was the theatre's own electrical generating plant, long since gone. The now vanished houses on the opposite side were mainly of the two storey variety and were largely let as tenements in the last century. Goldbeating, barometer making and printing were the main 18th century activities.

Post Box, Wellington Quay.
All boxes prior to 1922 bear the royal insignia of the era. "V.R." represents Queen Victoria up to 1901, "E.R." is King Edward VII who ruled from 1901 to 1910 and finally "G.R." for George V, 1910 to Independence in 1922. After 1922 the royal red colour of the pillars was changed to green.

TEMPLE BAR

Origin of name: Sir William Temple and Temple Bar, London (see introduction).

Irish name: Barra an Teampaill.

Former spelling: Temple Barr.

Date laid down: 1660's.

Development: In Bernard de Gomme's map of 1673 Temple Bar is shown and further land North of it is already reclaimed from the river.

Until the building of Carlisle (O'Connell) Bridge in 1794-1798 there were two ferry crossings from Temple Bar, one at the bottom of Temple Lane and another called Bagnio Slip (see Fownes Street, page 131).

Violin making, as already noted, was a widespread activity in the area and Temple Bar itself was no exception. Mr Petrie, a well-known fiddle manufacturer, worked from here. He died in 1771.

Eighteenth Century taverns we know to have existed in the area were the "Barbers Pole", the "Horse-shoe" and the "Magpie".

Activity on the street in the eighteenth century was extremely varied. Apart from taverns and some coffee houses a citizen could call on a cooper, a feather merchant, two shoemakers, three hatters, a shipbroker, a perukemaker, a watchmaker, a glazier and an oyle colour and dye seller. Today's clientele are more likely to be less hurried and more reflective as they visit the street's several restaurants and an art gallery or two.

Temple Bar

TEMPLE LANE SOUTH

Origin of name: Named (1750's) after the street Temple Bar.

Irish name: Lána an Teampaill Teas

Former names: Hogges Lane (circa 1577), Dirty Lane (1720's)

Date laid down: Mid 16th century.

Development: Originally little more than a dirty lane, (hence the second appellation) it had to wait until the 18th century for some significant building which included well constructed examples of brick warehouses and stables.

    The entrance to the pit of the Theatre Royal in Crow Street (this part of Crow Street was later renamed Cecilia Street) was from Temple Lane and conveniently adjacent to the very popular "Shakespeare Tavern".

    At the lower end of Temple Lane, before Wellington Quay was built in 1816, there was a Liffey ferry landing stage.

Sign of the Times

GENUINE EAU DE LUCE

As imported from Paris.

Is sold only by James Hoey, at the Mercury in Parliament-street, Price 1s. 7d. the bottle. This Eau de Luce is as much superior to what is commonly sold under that Name, as a Diamond is to a common Pebble, of which everyone will be convinced who shall make the Comparison.

To those who are unacquainted with its excellent Properties, it may not be important to mention that it has long been in the highest Estimation as a Smelling Bottle, in England, in France, and Ireland; that it is infinitely stronger that any Kind of Salts, more fragrant and refreshing than either Lavender, Hungary or any odoriferous Water. It recovers immediately from either Fainting or Historic Fits, and is a most admirable Remedy in the Head Ach, Lowness of Spirits, Hypochondriacal and Nervous Disorders.

The Freeman's Journal 19 — 21 November 1776.

GENTLEMEN,

There being a vacancy in parliament, by the Death of your later representative, Sir James Somerville Bart. I entreat the Favour of your Votes and Interests to succeed him, I am, with great respect, Gentlemen, your most faithful, most humble, and most obedient Servant,

JAMES DIGGES LATOUCHE

The Citizen's Journal 14 — 21 October 1749.

WELLINGTON QUAY

Origin of name: From Arthur Wellesley, Duke of Wellington, to celebrate his victory at Waterloo in 1815.

Irish version: Cé Wellington.

Date laid down: 1816.

Development: Wellington Quay was the last waterfront to be developed West of the new Custom House. Crampton and Aston Quays were already in existence but it was not possible to drive straight down to Essex Quay without diverting via Temple Bar and Essex Street. Up to this, houses built along this stretch of the river had their backs facing the water. The Wide Streets Commissioners bought up the necessary land and completed the Quay in 1816.

Solicitors and opticians were attracted to Wellington Quay from the earliest days and are still there in substantial numbers.

The Gallery of Photography, opened in 1978, is the only gallery in the country exclusively devoted to the exhibition and promotion of photography.

FIELD MARSHAL
ARTHUR DUKE OF WELLINGTON,
EMBASSADOR EXTRAORDINARY AND PLENIPOTENTIARY TO THE COURT OF FRANCE.
COLONEL OF THE ROYAL REGIMENT OF HORSE GUARDS,
DUKE OF CIUDAD RODRIGO IN SPAIN, DUKE OF VITTORIA IN PORTUGAL, &c.&c.&c.

Arthur Wellesley (1769-1852.)
Born in Dublin and created Duke of Wellington after his campaign in the Iberian Peninsula, he brought about the abdication of Napoleon in 1814. Wellesley defeated Napoleon at Waterloo and was British Prime Minister (1828 — 1830).

WELLINGTON QUAY

Henry Shaw's New City Pictorial Directory 1850

Sign of the Times

SHIP

TO BE SOLD, the Brig Samuel of Belfast, James McWaters, Master, now lying at George's-quay, opposite George's-street, with a Broom at her Mast Head. She is a new Vessel about 110 Tons Burthen, but eighteen months built, draws an easy Draught of Water, and is a remarkable good Sailor. The Inventory to be seen on Board. Proposals will be received for her by Mr Rowland Norris and Mr Folliot Magrath in Fleet-street, or Robert and Thomas Pettigrew in Linenhall Street, Dublin, March 21, 1777.

The Freeman's Journal 27 — 29 March 1777.

THE CLARENCE HOTEL AND DOLLARD HOUSE

Both these buildings stand on the site of the old Custom House. Dollard House itself is very reminiscent of the design of the Custom House which was erected in 1707.

Dollard House was originally Dollard Printers who established here in 1856 and have since moved to the suburbs as Brindley Dollard. When building Dollard's the black limestone first course of the Custom House was found at a depth of four and a half feet (1.4 metres). An old advertisement recounts that the Dollard Printing House made counter check books which were "Irish from start to finish and made in Dublin by Irish Trade Union Labour".

The Clarence Hotel is a noble survivor when other hotels close to it including the Dolphin and Jury's closed or fled the area. It was an hotel where traditions were and to some extent are still sacred.

In 1904 a room cost two shillings and you could have a fire in your room all day. In 1865 breakfast cost nine pence. Many commanding officers of the Anti-Treaty forces were staying in the hotel in June 1922 from where they had a clear view of the opening attack on the Four Courts. They speedily departed to join their units.

The present building dates from 1939. The hotel can also be entered from Essex Street East.

WESTMORELAND STREET
(West side)

Origin of name: From the Earl of Westmoreland.

Irish name: Sráid Fheistí (Street of the tidy-up or clearance).

Former name: Fleet Lane.

Date laid down: 1801.

In the 1700's there was a narrow road called Fleet Lane which extended from College Green to Fleet Street and then continued on, even narrower, to the river as Fleet Alley. It must be remembered that there was no bridge here until 1798 when Carlisle (O'Connell) Bridge was opened.

Westmoreland Street, along with D'Olier Street was the last major scheme carried out by the Wide Streets Commissioners. It was planned by Harry Aaron Baker (1753-1836). Some of the early 19th century buildings still survive but more were demolished to make way for worthy Victorian replacements. A number of 19th century alterations have been less successful.

Dublin's last street tram departed the Westmoreland Street Ballast Office at 12.45 pm on the 11th July 1949.

Power, the publishers of "Moore's Melodies", had its premises on Westmoreland Street.

John Fane,
10th Earl of Westmoreland,
Lord Lieutenant 1790-94.

His Excellency John Fane, Earl of WESTMORLAND, Lord Lieutenant General and General Governor of IRELAND.

Beshoff's, Westmoreland Street.
Beshoff's famous Fish and Chip Shop carries out its business in an ornate building. The founder of the firm, who died only recently, was Ivan Beshoff who took part in the famous mutiny on the Russian battleship, Potemkin, in 1905.

ROBINSON AND BUSSELL,
SUCCESSORS TO WILLIS AND CO.,
Pianoforte, Music, and Musical Instrument Warehous
MUSIC PUBLISHERS,
MILITARY MUSICAL INSTRUMENT MANUFACTURERS,
ROYAL HARMONIC SALOON, 7, WESTMORELAND-STREE
DUBLIN.

ianofortes and Harps for Hire, by the Week, Night, or Month Roman and English Strings—Fo
and English Guitars, Accordions, &c., &c., &c.

Robinson and Bussell, Westmoreland Street.
The premises of Robinson and Bussell, music warehouses and music instrument makers to the army. The building was demolished in 1887 for the new premises of the Northern Assurance Company.

145

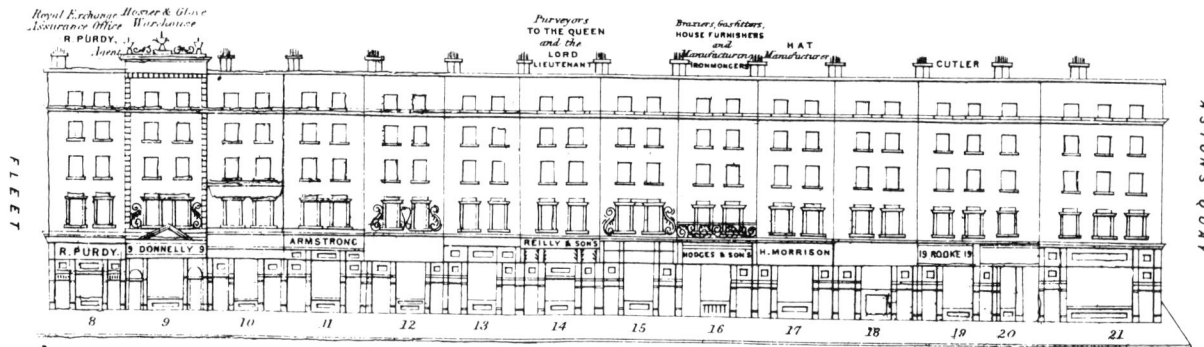

Henry Shaw's New City Pictorial Directory 1850

Sign of the Times

NEW SILKS
No.14 Parliament-street.

Thomas Collins begs leave to inform the Nobility, gentry, his Friends and the Public, that he has now completed his GREAT COLLECTION of new Winter Silks.

N.B. The Ladies will please to observe, that by purchasing at his House, they will avoid the great Inconvenience attending their shopping in narrow, disagreeable Streets, as the Approaches to Parliament-street are open and easy of Access.

The Freeman's Journal 14 — 16 October 1777.

BIBLIOGRAPHY

The Annals of DUBLIN —Fair City—, E.E. O'Donnell, Wolfhound Press, Dublin 1987.

The Book of the LIFFEY, editor. Elizabeth Healy, Wolfhound Press, Dublin 1988.

DUBLIN, Peter Somerville-Large, Granada Publishing Ltd., London 1979.

Dublin 1660-1860, Maurice Craig, Allen Figgis & Co. Ltd., Dublin 1980.

Dublin, Desmond Clarke, B.T. Batsford Ltd., Dublin 1977.

Dublin Historical Record, Old Dublin Society.

Encyclopaedia of DUBLIN, Douglas Bennett, Gill & Macmillan Ltd., Dublin 1991.

Guide to Historic Dublin, Adrian MacLoughlin, Gill & Macmillan Ltd., Dublin 1979.

A History of the City of Dublin, John T. Gilbert, Irish University Press 1972.

Lost Dublin, Frederick O'Dwyer, Gill & Macmillan Ltd., Dublin 1977.

The New City Pictorial Directory, 1850, Shaw, Dublin 1850.

Quakers in Eustace St., Becker & Pim, The Friendly Press, Dublin 1985.

Thom's Street Directories — Thom's Directories Ltd.

Mss. "The Archaeology of Viking Dublin", by Dr. Pat Wallace.

Mss. "Merchants' Hall", by Douglas Hyde.

Mss. "Aspects of the History of The Temple Bar Area", by Sean Murphy.

Extracts from "The Freeman's Journal", The Gilbert Library, Dublin.

Extracts from "The Citizen's Journal", The Gilbert Library, Dublin.

Illustration Credits:

The National Library 9, 22, 23, 25, 26, 27, 34, 35, 37, 38, 43, 50, 51, 70, 75, 82, 89, 92, 120, 123, 128, 130, 141, 144.

The Irish Architectural Archive 78, 83, 90, 96, 135, 142, 145, 146.

Dublin Corporation Archives 36.

Glenn Thompson 42.

The National Gallery 37, 101, 110.

INDEX

A

Abbey Street, Lower, 118
Act of Union, 35, 51, 54, 55, 85, 87
Adair, Sir Robert, 74
Adair Lane, 74
Ahern family, 60
Alan McShane Ltd., **55**
Alex Thom & Co., 95
All Hallows Priory, 22, 83
Allied Irish Banks, Foster Place, 58-9, 68, 72
Anglesea, 1st Earl of, 75, 127
Anglesea Street, 51, 61, 75-6, 84, 107
    Stock Exchange, 97
Anglo-Normans, 19-20
Annesley, Arthur, 1st Earl of Anglesea, 75, 127
Annesley, Francis, Viscount Valentia, 75
Apothecaries Hall, Company of the, 82
archaeological excavations, 16
Asdill, John, 74
Asdill's Row, 74
Ashlin, G. C., 62
Aston, Henry, 78
Aston Place, 74, 77, 129
Aston Quay, 47, 72, 74, 78-9, 100, 129, 141
Ath Cliath, 11, 12
Atkinson, Richard, 108
Augustinian Hermits, Order of, 81

B

Bad Ass Cafe, 99
Bad Bob's, 118
Bagnio Slip, 131, 139
"Baite," 116
Baker, Harry Aaron, 144
Ball Alley, 94
Ballast Office, 72, 144
Ballybough Bridge, 54
Bank of Ireland, College Green, 87, 98
    Armoury, 64, 106, 134
    Cash Office, 42
    Coat of Arms, 41
    Yeomanry, 42
"Barbers Pole" tavern, 139
Barry, Kevin, 129
Barry, Spranger, 82
Bear Tavern, 93
Beckett, J. W., 74
Beckett, Samuel, 100
Bedford, 4th Duke of, 80
Bedford Lane, 80
Bedford Row, 80, 104
Bellingham, Sir Daniel, 30
Beshoff, Ivan, 145
Beshoff's Fish and Chip Shop, 145
Bewley, Joshua, 111, 138
Bewley family, 125
Bewley's Cafe, Westmoreland St, 111, 137
Bewley's Chambers, 129
Black Death, 21
Blind Gate, 113

Blind Quay, 52, 89, 116, 120, 126
Bloom's Hotel, 76
bollards, 46
Borace, Sir John, 84
Bothe Street, 127
Bourke, Patrick J., 114
Boyle, Richard, 1st Earl of Cork, 90
Bradogue river, 94
Bride's Alley, 125
Bridewell, the, 27
Bridge Street, 125
Brindley Dollard, 143
Bristol, 19, 22
Bronze Age, 11, 12
Brookings Map, 1728, 75
Bruce, Edward, 21
Burgh Quay, 78
Burke and Cavendish, assassination of, 138
Butler family, 52
Buttevant's Tower, 115, 126, 136
Byrne, John F., 112, 119

C

Cadogan's Alley, 120
Cahill, Catherine, 47
Campbell, Patrick, 111
Campbell Catering, 111
Capel, Arthur, Earl of Essex, 117, 120
Capel Street, 29
Carey's Hospital, 27
Carlisle Bridge, 92, 139, 144
Carlton, Alderman, 102
Case's Tower, 126
Cassels, Richard, 35
Castle Street, 23, 89, 128, 132
Cathair Books, 115
Catholic Boy Scouts of Ireland, 131
Catholic Emancipation, 102
Catholic University School of Medicine, 81, 82
Cecilia House, 81
Cecilia Street, 81-2, 95, 140
Central Bank, Dame Street, 64, 81, 88, 106, 131, 138
    "Crann an Oir," 114
Ceppi, Peter, and Sons, 112
Chain of Office (Lord Mayor), 30
Chaplin, Charlie, 57
Charles II, King, 28, 123
Chebsey's Glass Works, 54
Chester, 22
Chichester House, 27, 84, 87
Christ Church Cathedral, 13, 24, 34, 35, 44, 132
Christ Church Place, 132
    excavations, 16
Christianity, coming of, 13-14
C.I.E., 71
Cill Cele Crist (Christ Church Cathedral), 13
City Hall, 97, 108, 126
City Hall Inn, 138
City of Dublin Workingmen's Club, 44

City Seal, 24
City Stocks, 24
City Sword, 24, 30
City Walls, 20
Civic Museum, 42
Clarence Hotel, 31, 143
Clarendon Street, 95
Cleary and Doyle, 125
Cleghorn, George, 123
Clohissy's Bookshop, 80
Clonliffe House, 82
coal covers, 45
Coalbrookdale, Shropshire, 66
Coat of Arms, 45
coins, 29
Cole's Alley, 125
College Green, 22, 41, 43, 49, 51, 70, 113, 129, 134, 144
    history of, 83-5
    Malton view, 37
College Street, 131
Commercial Buildings, 39, 91, 94, 97
Cook, Andrew, 89
Cooke, John J., & Son, 81
Cooley, Thomas, 76
Cope, Robert, 88
Cope Street, 88, 94
Copper Alley, 28, 88-9
Cork, 1st Earl of, 28, 90
Cork Hill, 28, 90, 126, 132
Courtney & Stephens, 59
Cowle, Jack, 52
Cramer & Co., Messrs., 62
Crampton, Philip, 36, 91, 92
Crampton Buildings, 74
Crampton Court, 56, 91, 92
Crampton Quay, 92, 100, 108, 141
Crane Lane, 52, 86, 93, 118
"Crann an Oir," 114
Cromwellian Wars, 28
Crow, William, 95
Crow Street, 66, 81, 95, 140
Crow Street Theatre, 33, 81, 82, 95
Crowe & Sons, 59
Crown Alley, 65, 94, 99
    Telephone Exchange, 63
Crow's Nest, 95
Cruise, Jack, 57
Currency Commission, 106
Custom House, 28, 34, 36, 117, 141
Custom House, Old, 34, 37, 93, 119, 126
Custom House Printing House, 117
Custom House Quay, 31, 52, 92, 93, 117

D

Dalkey Island, 11
Daly, Patrick, 51
Daly's Club, 51-2, 84, 130
Damas Street, 113
Dame Street, 27, 41, 43, 52, 56, 69, 91, 97, 123, 131, 132
    1753, 38
    1850, 96

Central Bank building, 64
  history of, 29, 113-14
  1790's, 101
  widened, 33, 36
Dame's Gate, 27, 113
Darley, Frederick, 108
Davis, O'Connor and Company, 74
Davis, Thomas, 85
de Clare, Richard FitzGilbert, 19
de Gomme, Bernard, 139
De Gomme-Phillips map, 1685, 75
Deane, Sir Thomas, & Son, 63
Deane and Woodworth, 69
Delaney, Edward, 85
Derricke, John, 26
Dillon & Waldron, 61
Dirty Lane, 140
Division Bell, House of Commons, 54
Dodder river, 94
D'Olier Street, 15, 144
Dollard House, 143
Dollard Printers, 143
Dollard Printing House, 118
Dolphin Hotel, 47, 117, 118, 143
Dolphin House, 117
Dubh Linn (Black Pool), 13, 16
Dublin
  Anglo-Norman, 19-20
  Coat of Arms, 45
  early Christian, 13-14
  Middle Ages, 21-5
  prehistory, 11-13
  regalia, 24, 30
  20th c., 68
  16th century, 25-6
  17th century, 28-31
  18th century, 33-9
  19th century, 41-66
  Viking, 15-18
Dublin Academy of Music, 82
Dublin Artisans' Dwelling Company, 74
"Dublin Builder," 59
Dublin Castle, 14, 18, 23, 25, 26, 33, 36,
  90, 126, 136
  Fenian Rising, 31
Dublin Chamber of Commerce, 39
Dublin City Mission, 108
Dublin Corporation, 20, 24, 57, 63, 66,
  68, 116, 132
  electricity supply, 104
  Preservation List, 97
Dublin Corporation Cultural Envir-
  onment Award, 1981, 61
"Dublin Gazette," 117
"Dublin Journal," 117, 136
Dublin Metropolitan District Court, 117
"Dublin Penny Journal," 81
Dublin Philosophical Society, 95
Dublin Resource Centre, 95
Dublin Stock Exchange, 76, 97
Dublin Volunteers, 39
Dublin Working Boys' Home and Hard-
ing Technical School, 132
"Dutch Billy" houses, 29, 30, 38
"Dyflin" the, 17

E
Eagle Tavern, Cork Hill, 90
"Eagle" tavern, Eustace St, 39, 123
East Wall Watersports Group, 17
Easter Rising, 1916, 63, 95, 129, 133
Eden Quay, 129
Electric Lighting Company, 104
Electricity Supply Board (ESB), 80, 104-
5
Empire Theatre of Varieties, 56-7
Essex, Earl of, 116, 117, 120
Essex Bridge, 29, 34, 36, 37, 116, 136
Essex Gate, 115, 136
Essex Quay, 116, 141
Essex Street, 31, 47, 49, 141
  East, 91, 112, 117-19, 143
  West, 89, 103, 115, 119-22, 126
Eucharistic Congress, 112
Eustace, Sir Maurice, 123
Eustace Street, 48, 119, 123-5
"Evening Mail," 107
Exchange Buildings, 132
Exchange Hotel, 136
Exchange Street, 52, 126
  Lower, 102, 105, 116, 120
  Upper, 89

F
Faddle Alley, 94
Fane, John, 10th Earl of Westmoreland,
  144
Faulkner, George, 117, 136
Fenians, 31, 136
Fenton, Lady Alice, 88
Fenton, Sir Geoffrey, 88
Fingal, 15
Fionn Gaill, the, 15
Fire Brigade, 49
Fishamble Street, 23, 89, 116, 127-8
  excavations, 16, 18
  explosion, 1596, 22
  No. 26, 105
Fishamble Street Music Hall, 33, 34, 89,
  103, 127, 128
Fitzgeralds, Westmoreland Street, 46
Fleet Alley, 144
Fleet Lane, 144
Fleet Street, 31, 74, 77, 129, 130, 144
  Power Station, 104, 105
Foley, John Henry, 85
Foot, Lundy, 136
footscrapers, 45
Foras Aiseanna Saothair (FAS), 116
Forbes Ross, 93
Ford of the Hurdles, 11, 12
Foster, John, 55, 130
Foster Place, 36, 38, 51, 64, 68, 70, 72,
  106, 107
  Allied Irish Banks, 58-9
  history of, 130
Fownes, Cecilia, 81
Fownes, Elizabeth, 88
Fownes, Sir William, 88, 131
Fownes Court, 39, 138
Fownes Street, 38, 69, 81, 131

Fownes Street Buildings, 55
"Freeman's Journal," 86, 93
Fyssche Slyppe, Fishamble St, 17

G
Gaiety Theatre, 54, 57
Gandon, James, 87
General Post Office, 128, 138
Geneva Conference Agreement, 1954,
  129
Gentlemen, Kerry Association of, 39
Geoghegan, Charles, 59
George I, King, 34
Georgian period, 33-9
Gibbs, Robert, 42
Glasnevin, 13
Globe Coffee House, 117
Gokstad ship, 17
Gough, General Viscount Hugh, 85
Grace, butcher, 80
Grand Canal Street, 116
Grattan, Henry, 85, 127
Grattan Bridge, 28
Gray, Murray and Associates, 112
Great Brunswick Street, 97
Great Hunger, 125
Great Mace, 30
Griffith, Arthur, 131
Guard House, Bank of Ireland, 106, 130
Guild of Cooks, 39
Guild of Cutlers, 52
Guilds, 24
Guinness, Arthur, 52
Guinness, Richard, 52

H
Halfpenny Bridge, 17, 50, 66
Hall, James, 60
Hamilton, Hugh Douglas, 95
Hammond & Co., Messrs., 104
Handel, G. F., 34, 103
Hanna, Fred, 100
Harding Technical School, 48, 132
Hasculf, King, 19
Haughton family, 125
Hawkins Street, 78
Hell Fire Club, 90
Henry II, King, 19
Henry VIII, King, 25, 95
Hibernian Insurance Company, 69
Hibernian United Services Club, 130
High Street
  excavations, 16
Hodges Hardware, 79
Hogg, William, & Co., 55, 76
Hoggen Green, 22, 25, 83
Hogges Lane, 140
Holy Faith Sisters, 95
Holy Trinity, Fraternity of the, 108
Holy Trinity friary, 124
Horse Guard Yard, 91
"Horse-shoe" tavern, 139
House of Commons, 54, 55, 98
House of Lords, 54, 98
Huguenots, 29

I

Indecon House, Wellington Quay, 112
Invincibles, 138
"Ireland a Nation," 114
"Iris Oifigiúil," 117
"Irish Builder," 62
Irish Continental Line, 79
Irish Film Centre, 125
Irish Free Masons, Grand Masters Lodge of, 39
"Irish Melodies" (Moore), 144
"Irish People," 136
Irish Shipping, 79
Irish Trade Union Trust, 129
Irish Women Workers' Union, 129
Isod's Lane, 126
Isolde's Tower, 116, 126

J

Jacob family, 125
James Flynn & Co., 61
James II, King, 29, 117
Jervis, Sir Humphrey, 29
John, King, 20
Johnston, Francis, 42, 51, 87
Jones, Frederick E. "Buck," 82
Jone's Road, 82
Joyce, James, 76, 80, 100, 112, 119, 133
Jury's Hotel, 84, 143
Jury's Hotel Group, 76

K

Kearney, Peadar, 57
Kennan & Sons, Ironworks, 35, 103, 120
Kinlay, Howard, 132
Kinlay House, 132
Kirk, Joseph R., 106

L

Lambay Island, 15
languages, 20
Laurel and Hardy, 57
Lee's Lane, 77
Lennon's, 133
Lever Brothers, 109
Leverhulme, Lord, 109
Liffey Bridge, 66
Liffey Dockyard, 17
Liffey river, 11, 13, 15, 17, 27, 123, 124, 138
    land reclamation, 20, 31
Lighton, Sir Thomas, 58
Lighton's Bank, 58, 130
Liptons, 123
Liverpool, 22
Lockwood, Margaret, 57
longships, 15, 17
Lord Edward Street, 41, 48, 89, 90, 128, 132
Lord Mayor's Chain, 30
Lords Deputy, 25
Lowry, Dan, 56
Lucas' Coffee House, 90
Lundy Foot & Co., 115, 136

M

McAuley, Catherine, 89
McBirney, Collis & Co., 79
McBirney's Stores, 47, 137
Mace, House of Commons, 55
McKeever & Son, 107
MacMurrough, Dermot, 19
McShane, Alan, Ltd, 55
"Magpie" tavern, 139
Maguire, Betty, 116
Malton, James, 37, 101, 110
Mangan, James Clarence, 127
manhole covers, 137
Manley, Isaac, 138
maps
    Speed's Map, 1610, 27, 28
    Temple Bar, c 1816, 40
    Temple Bar, c. 1750, 32
    Temple Bar, c. 1900, 67
    Temple Bar, present day, 73
Mary's Abbey, 98
Mason Instruments, 109
Mayor, the, 30
Mayor of Dublin, 24
Meath Street, 125
Merchant Tailor's School, 108
Merchants' Arch, 133
Merchants' Guild, 108, 133
Merchants' Hall, 108
Merchants' Quay, 11, 22, 34
Mercier & Co., 76
mesolithic period, 11
"Messiah" (Handel), 35, 103
Metal Bridge, 66
Metropole Hotel, 104
Meyers, George, 97
Middle Ages, 21-5
Millennium, Dublin, 116
Miller & Symes, Messrs., 97
Molyneux, Daniel, 45
Moore, Thomas, 76, 144
Moses, Marcus, 62
Mulvany Brothers, 112
Municipal Corporation Reform Act, 108
Munster and Leinster Bank, 58
Murray, Albert E., 132
Murray & Co., 61
Murray, William G., 62
Music Hall, Fishamble Street, 33, 34, 89, 103, 127, 128

N

Nantes, Edict of, 29
National Telephone Company, 63
Neal, William, 35
Needham, Thomas, 58
New Street, 123
Newman, Jacob, 123
Noonan Shirt Manufacturer, 108
Norseman Public House, 119
North Frederick Street, 131
Northern Assurance Company, 62, 145
Nugent, Michael, 47, 117, 118

O

O'Callaghan, J. J., 117
O'Casey, Sean, 100
O'Connell, Daniel, 102
O'Connell Bridge, 92, 139, 144
O'Connell Street, 36, 138
O'Dea, Jimmy, 57, 114
O'Doherty, Eamonn, 114
O'Donnell and Twomey, 125
O'Donovan, Harry, 114
Ogilby, John, 29, 120
O'Hurley, Dermot, Archbishop of Cashel, 25
Olaf, St, 127
Old Custom House, 34, 37, 93, 119, 126
Old Guard House, Bank of Ireland, 106, 130
Oldham, John, 98
O'Leary, John, 100
Olympia Theatre, 56-7, 91, 111, 113, 138
Oman's warehouse, 65, 94
Orange Street, 120
O'Reilly's Fine Art Auction Rooms, 107
Ormonde, Duke of, 29, 75, 123
Ostmen, 15
"Ouzel", the, 39
Ouzel Galley Society, 39

P

Palace Bar, 60
Parke, Robert, 87
Parliament House, 27, 33, 36, 51, 54-5, 87, 98, 130. see also Bank of Ireland, College Green
Parliament Row, 134
Parliament Street, 33, 34, 36, 37, 47, 52, 90, 136
    archaeological site, 11
    1790's, 110
    Sunlight Chambers, 109
Patrick, St, 13
Pearce, Sir Edward Lovett, 54, 87
Pearse Street, 15, 97
Penal Laws, 29, 102, 125
Perot, Anne, 75
Perry, Thomas, 76
Petrie, Mr, 139
Phoenix Park, 123, 138
Photography, Gallery of, 141
Pigeon House Fort, 104
Pim family, 125
Playhouse, Capel St, 82
Poddle river, 13, 31, 94, 113, 123, 124, 138
Porter's Row, 80
"Portrait of the Artist as a Young Man" (Joyce), 112
post boxes, 138
Power, Tyrone, 57
Power publishers, 144
Presbyterian School, 125
Presbyterians, 123
Preston's Lane, 88
Price's Lane, 74, 137
"Prince of Wales" theatre, 35

Project Arts Centre, 118
Provincial Bank of Ireland, 58
"Punch Bowl", the, 123

Q
Quakers, 39, 123, 125
Queen's Theatre, 114

R
Rathborne Wax Chandlers, 91, 117
RDS Art School, 85
Read & Co., 52-3
Read, Elizabeth, 52
Read, James, 52
Read, John, 53
Red Lion Tavern, 89
Reformation, the, 25
Reilly, Michael, & Co., 107
Religious Society of Friends. *see* Quakers
Restoration Period, 28-31
Reynolds, Thomas, 131
Richmond Street, 97
"Riding the Franchises," 24, 108
Robinson and Bussell, 145
Rock Garden, 65
Roe, Paddy, 98
Rosemary Lane, 102
Rotunda Cinema, 114
Rover car showrooms, 132
Rowntree-Mackintosh, 103
Royal Assurance Company, 137
Royal Bank, 58
    porter's bell, 72
    Roll of Honour, 68
Royal Dublin Society, 95
Royal Exchange, 90, 108, 126
Royal Exchange Coffee House, 97
Royal Hospital, Donnybrook, 129
Royal Hospital, Kilmainham, 34
Royal Liver Building, Aston Quay, 72
Royal Liver Friendly Society, 72
Royal Mint, 29
Russell, John, 4th Duke of Bedford, 80
Rutherford, Margaret, 57

S
Sackville Street, 36, 138
St Anne's Church, Dawson St, 132
St Audoen's Arch, Cork St, 20
St Audoen's church, 14
St Augustine, monastery of, 95
St Brigid's Well, 27
St Colum Cille, church of, 13-14
St Doulagh's church, 14
St Mac Tail's church, 14
St Mark's parish, 78
St Martin's church, 14
St Mary de Hogge, convent of, 83
St Mary del Dam, church of, 90, 113
St Nicholas Street, 125
St Nicholas' within the walls parish, 102
St Olaf's church, 14
St Patrick's Cathedral, 13, 35
St Tulloch's Lane, 127
St Werburgh's Church, 49
St Werburgh's parish, 102

St Winifred's Well, 124
Sts Michael and John, church of, 102, 120
    bell, 49
Sandford, John, 60
"Sans Pareil Theatre, The," 35
Saul's Court, 128
Scarlet Alley, 126
Scout Shop, 131
Scouting Association of Ireland, 76
Sculptors' Society of Ireland, 116
setts, stone, 46
"Shakespeare Tavern," 140
Shamrock Chambers, Eustace St, 48
Shaw, George Bernard, 100
Shaw, Robert, 58
Shaw's New City Pictorial Directory, 1850, 78, 83, 86, 90, 142, 146
Shelbourne Hotel, 104
"Ship", the, 123
Sidney, Sir Henry, 26
Sinn Féin, 131
Sir Patrick Dun's Hospital, 116
Sir Thomas Carey's Hospital, 84
Sisters of Mercy, 89
Sitric II, King, 16
Skin the Goat, 138
Skinner's Row, 132
Smock Alley, 82, 89, 120
Smock Alley Theatre, 29, 33, 102, 120-2
Smyth, Edward, 87, 98
Solidarity House, 129
South Great George's Street, 111
Sparks, Isaac, 76
Speed, John, 27, 28, 120
Speed's Map, 1610, 27, 28, 120, 127
Stable Lane, 120
Stamp Office of Ireland, 123
Star of Erin Music Hall, 56
Steine river, 83
Stenor's Vulcanising Machines, 112
Stephenson Gibney and Associates, 64
Stock Exchange, Anglesea Street, 97, 107
Stocks, 24
Strangeways, Leonard R., 120
Strongbow (Richard de Clare), 19
Suffolk Street
    archaeological site, 11
Sullivan, T. D., 132
Sunlight Chambers, 109
Survey of the Fortified Irish Lands, 95
Swift, Dean Jonathan, 117, 138
Sycamore Alley, 111, 123, 125, 138
Sycamore Street, 138

T
Talbot Street, 88
Tallaght, 13
Taylor, J., 102
Telephone Exchange, Crown Alley, 63
Temple, John, 131
Temple, Sir William, 9, 139
Temple Bar
    churches, 13-14
    name of, 9, 139

Temple Bar, maps of
    c.1900, 67
    c. 1200, 19
    c. 1610, 21
    c. 1750, 32
    c. 1816, 40
    c. 800 A.D., 13
    Middle Ages, 21
    present day, 73
    Viking period, 15
Temple Lane, 44, 139, 140
Temple Lane Studios, 71
Teyngmouth Stret, 113
Theatre Royal, 54, 66, 82, 140
Thingmote Street, 113
Tholsel, the, 23
Thomas Read & Co., 52-3
Thom's Directories, 95
Thorndyke, Sybil, 57
Three Candles Print, 77
"Three Stags Heads", the, 123
Thundercut Alley, 94
trams, 144
Traynor, Thomas, 133
Trinity College, 13, 22, 27, 38, 56, 83-4, 113, 127
Trinity Street, 83, 113
Turnstile Alley, 130, 134
Tyrrel, Walter, 95

U
U. S. Information Service, 129
U.B.S. Bank, Switzerland, 84
"Ulysses" (Joyce), 76, 80, 133
Union of Students in Ireland (USI), 77
"United Irishman," 131
United Irishmen, 39
USIT, 79, 132
Ussher, James, 127

V
van Beaver, John, 54
van der Hagen, Johann, 54
Vestment Warehouse, Parliament Street, 47
Vikings, 15-18
Virgin Megastore, 47, 79

W
Waldron, Laurence, Ambrose & Co., 61
Walpole family, 125
Walsh, William, 66
Ward, John, 77
water pumps, 49
Webb family, 125
Webb's Bookshop, 100
Wellington, Duke of, 141
Wellington Quay, 31, 33, 36, 37, 44, 131, 140
    history of, 41, 92, 141-3
    Indecon House, 112
    post box, 138
    right-of-way, 133
    1820's, 50
Wentworth, Sir Thomas, 28
Werburgh Street, 120

Westbury Hotel, 95
Westmoreland, 10th Earl of, 144
Westmoreland Street, 33, 36, 41, 43, 62, 111, 129, 144-6
"Whigs of the Capital," 39
Whitelaw's census, 1798, 78
Wide Streets Commissioners, 33, 36, 38, 108, 113, 130, 133, 136, 141, 144
Wilde, Oscar, 100
Wilkinson, William, 76

William Hogg & Co., 55
William III, of Orange, King, 29, 30, 85, 117
Wilson's Directory, 1762, 80
Wilson's Street Directory, 1762, 128
Windsor, John, 66
Winetavern Street, 16, 22
Winifred, St, 124
Wiro, St, bishop of Dublin, 14
Woffington, Peg, 120

Wood Quay, 116, 126
  excavations, 17
World War I, 68
Wormwood Gate, 125

Y
Yeats, W. B., 100
Yeomanry, 42
Yorkshire Insurance Company, 49